A **FALCON** GUIDE

Toproping

D0010940

A CHOCKSTONE PRESS BOOK

FALCON®
HELENA, MONTANA

S. Peter Lewis
how to rock climb series

Developed by Chockstone Press

Falcon Press Publishing Co, Inc.
P.O. Box 1718
Helena, Montana 59624

Toproping
© 1998 S. Peter Lewis
All rights reserved. Published 1998
Printed in the United States of America.

COVER: Doug Skiba on *Brain Cloud (9)*, Golden Cliffs, Colorado.

Library of Congress Cataloging-in-Publication Data

Lewis, S. Peter
  Toproping / S. Peter Lewis
    p. cm. – (How to rock climb series) (A Falcon guide)
  "A Chockstone Press book."
  Includes index.
  ISBN 1-56044-753-2
  1. Rock climbing.   I. Title.   II. Series.   III. Series: A Falcon
guide.
GV200 . 2 . L48   1998
796 . 52 ' 23–dc21   98-21199
                                                              CIP

To my friend Bob Clark for a belay anchor demonstration twenty years ago that scared me straight, and to my fellow guides in the White Mountains for continuing my education.

S. Peter

Toproping Deck Chairs on the Titanic (10a), Golden Cliffs.

C O N T E N T S

TOP-ROPING

S. PETER LEWIS

WARNING: CLIMBING IS A SPORT WHERE YOU MAY BE SERIOUSLY INJURED OR DIE

READ THIS BEFORE YOU USE THIS BOOK.

This is an instruction book for rock climbing, a sport which is inherently dangerous. You should not depend solely on information gleaned from this book for your personal safety. Your climbing safety depends on your own judgment based on competent instruction, experience, and a realistic assessment of your climbing ability.

There is no substitute for personal instruction in rock climbing and climbing instruction is widely available. You should engage an instructor or guide to learn climbing safety techniques. If you misinterpret a concept expressed in this book, you may be killed or seriously injured as a result of the misunderstanding. Therefore, the information provided in this book should be used only to supplement competent personal instruction from a climbing instructor or guide. Even after you are proficient in climbing safely, occasional use of a climbing guide is a safe way to raise your climbing standard and learn advanced techniques.

There are no warranties, either expressed or implied, that this instruction book contains accurate and reliable information. There are no warranties as to fitness for a particular purpose or that this book is merchantable. Your use of this book indicates your assumption of the risk of death or serious injury as a result of climbing's risks and is an acknowledgement of your own sole responsibility for your climbing safety.

Acknowledgements

No one writes a book like this relying only on their own knowledge. If I were to go back through this book looking for techniques that I had invented, I would come up empty handed. The principles and techniques in this book have been identified and refined by many climbers over many years—I have simply presented these ideas in a format that is easy to understand and apply. Though I have probably learned something from everyone I have ever climbed with, an exhaustive list isn't appropriate. I will take the time, however, to single out a few groups and individuals. Special thanks to:

My fellow guides in North Conway, for providing me with a learning environment where innovation and critical thinking are encouraged and where excellence is never good enough;

Marc Chauvin, whose energy and inventive spirit continues to mystify me—you can learn a lot from Marc just listening to him talk in his sleep;

Members of the American Mountain Guides Association Technical Committee, an information resource I have taken advantage of many times;

Alain Comeau, for helping me organize and present this information and for his encouragement;

The American Alpine Club for allowing me to use excerpts from *Accidents in North American Mountaineering;*

Heidi Skiba and Mike Maurer for help with the photos;

Several equipment manufacturers for their enthusiastic support of this project through product donation: Wild Country, Metolius, Petzl, Sterling Ropes, Black Diamond, Climb High, and Lowe Alpine;

And Doug Skiba, for never allowing me to get away with writing a sloppy sentence.

Heidi Skiba practices edging on a thin face. S. Peter Lewis

Introduction

Toproping seems so basic. For most climbers a toprope was their introduction to climbing. Though many climbers move on to traditional leading, sport climbing, bouldering or big walls, toproping is still a great way to get in a little climbing here and there.

It's so easy to grab a pitch after work, to get in a couple of laps early on a Saturday morning or to pull off the interstate on the way to Yosemite and try a new area mentioned in the magazines. With just a rope, a little equipment and a Crazy Creek™ chair you can spend a summer afternoon falling carefree off routes harder than you can do. You're never far from the ground, it's usually just a short walk to the car or the swimming hole, there's no exposure, and a fall is just a sag on the rope. On the surface toproping seems simple; just rig the rope, tie in, set up the belay, and start making moves. But beneath the surface run strong currents and a careless moment can catch the unwary like a swimmer dragged away in an undertow. Statistics tell us that most automobile accidents occur within five miles of home. In climbing it's likely that most accidents happen within one pitch of the ground.

Toproping relies on the foundational climbing skills of anchoring, belaying, rope handling and safety management. These skills are so basic to climbing that no one without them has ever gone on to climb the El Cap in a day, or the Trango Tower. As a result you would expect that the scene at the local toproping crag would be the perfect model of expertise, efficiency, and attentiveness. Unfortunately the opposite is often true.

Part of the problem can be attributed to climbing's public acceptance. A generation ago climbing was still mysterious. Look at a photo from back then and you'll see climbers laden with complicated equipment and dressed for battle. Every climb looked like an expedition and it was obvious that you needed to know something just to get started. Pick up a magazine today and you're likely to see a 14 year-old in a pair of tights clipping a few quickdraws on a plastic cliff at the mall. The mystery is gone; climbing is child's play—so they say.

In the introduction to the 1996 edition of *Accidents in North American Mountaineering,* the American Alpine Club publication that documents each year's climbing accidents, editor Jed Williamson points to an ominous trend:

"Everything goes in cycles, which in the case of causes for climbing accidents is unfortunate. Nothing cold be more illustrative of this than the category 'Rappel Failure/Error.' Last year there were twelve reports and this year there are fifteen that are attributed to rappel problems. They are mostly of a different nature than in the past, and at least half of them occurred on toprope climbs."

A quick look at the analysis of some of these toprope accidents demonstrates that lack of fundamental skills, failure to follow basic principles and a cavalier attitude are the main contributors.

"It appears that the rope or the anchor carabiner changed position, and the rope ran across the gate...and unclipped it."

"Considering Chris' unfamiliarity with rappelling, she should have been belayed.

"...the sling directly holding the rope had been melted through, almost certainly by the friction of the rope as the climbers were belayed and lowered."

"One (fatal accident) occurred when a man slipped and fell 60 feet to the road. He was setting up a toprope at the time."

In the spring of 1977 I held my first climbing fall. It was nearly my last. My partner and I were toproping a 5.6 climb at Ragged Mountain in Connecticut. I was at belaying at the top of the crag with my legs dangling over the side—without any anchor. My partner fell and nearly pulled me off. Driving home later we discussed our close call. We knew we had been stupid and wondered if there was a better way.

The next weekend we were back. I sat at the top of a steep 5.7 dihedral. Like the weekend before, my feet dangled over the edge and again I shouted "on belay" to my partner. But this time I thought I was smarter. On the walk up to the top I had found a Lost Arrow piton in the scree. While my partner tied in, I took a rock and drove the piton into the flat top of Ragged Mountain. Feeling terribly clever, I clipped into my harness with a sling. I assumed we were safe.

As my partner climbed another climber walked by. When we were done he introduced himself. His name was Bob Clark and he had been climbing at Ragged for years. "What's that?" he asked, pointing to the piton. "That's our anchor" I said proudly. Bob kicked the piton and it came out and skidded across the ground. He pointed toward the woods. "Use trees" he said.

That marked the beginning of my climbing education. I climbed with Bob several times and learned a lot. A few years later I moved to North Conway, NH and began working as a mountain guide. I guided on and off for a dozen years in the company of some of the country's best guides and continued up the learning curve.

Unfortunately during those years, I witnessed many close calls and a few tragedies.

One day, a pitch below the top of Cathedral Ledge, I heard sirens. I climbed to the summit with my clients and walked over to where another guide was peering over the edge. I could tell just by his posture that something really bad was happening. I stood next to him and looked over. Five hundred feet below I saw another guide kneeling on the ground over a fallen climber. I recognized the guide's helmet. "What's Marc doing?" I asked. There was a long pause then Jeff turned and looked at me. "CPR" he said quietly. I don't think either of us could have felt more helpless. Marc told us later that most of the dead climber's gear still had store stickers on it. He had fallen, caught his leg on the rope, flipped over and hit his head. He was twenty feet off the ground. If he'd been wearing a helmet he might have walked away.

I've watched climbers rappel off the end of their ropes, burn through anchor webbing, drop each other, smash into the cliff because they didn't think they needed an anchor on the ground, break bones on easy approaches, tie in wrong, clip in wrong, belay off anchors that fail under hand pressure, and nearly fall out of a rappel, all within one pitch of the ground. Some of them died.

What has amazed me most after all these years, is how preventable these accidents can be with education. This book is one educational tool I wish I had twenty years ago when I stepped gingerly onto the learning curve. In this sport you can't make very many little mistakes, they can add up to disaster. And a big mistake is often the last, and it doesn't really matter if you make it a hundred feet off the ground, or a thousand.

When climbers get together they like to trade horror stories. They laugh and quiver in mock terror as the stories are told, each eager to describe the times they cheated death. I hope this book gives climbers a lot less to talk about.

Getting off the ground at Squat Rock, South Platte, Colorado.

S. Peter Lewis

Getting Off The Ground

Of all the climbers who are on belay, many of them are toproping. Some are outdoors at their local crag having fun with friends in a relaxing atmosphere. Many are pushing their limits, seeing how hard a route they can do. Others are rehearsing routes for a future lead, or training by doing laps. Some are experiencing climbing for the very first time, while others are practicing placing gear. Meanwhile, indoor gyms are full of climbers improving technique and getting stronger.

Toproping appears so simple. It seems that all you need is the basic equipment and a little free time. But toproping's apparent simplicity is deceiving. When compared with multi-pitch, traditional climbing, toproping appears much less complicated. But the reality is, whether one pitch up or twenty, the practical application of climbing's fundamental principles and techniques is still required. It is frightening, however, how frequently people at the crags make fundamental mistakes that endanger themselves and others. Often it is obvious that they are unaware of their errors.

Climbing is dangerous. You can die. You can die toproping. But climbing is also challenging, fulfilling, and a whole lot of fun.

This book will introduce you to the fundamental principles, techniques, and systems used in toproping. Mastering these will build a foundation of skills and experience preparing you to lead, climb multipitch routes, and expand your climbing aspirations as far and high as you like. It will also teach you the basic safety management principles that will help you stay alive while you learn.

This book will not teach you how to make moves, look good, train, lead routes, or make the right judgment calls. Reading this book will not make you an expert: experiment on the ground until you feel confident that you can take the techniques to the cliffs.

HOW TO USE THIS BOOK

This book focuses on equipment, anchoring, belaying, and safety management. Each topic is divided into a basic and advanced chapter. How you use this book depends on your level of expertise and your climbing goals.

The chapters on basic equipment, basic toprope systems, and basic safety management introduce foundational systems but assume some climbing knowledge. (For example, they teach the use of specific knots but assume that the reader knows how to tie them, and they assume that the reader understands the basic mechanics of belaying). The basic chapters are designed for novices who have always climbed with a more experienced partner and now want to launch out on their own, or for the gym climber who would like to head outside. The basic chapters limit the climbing options to routes less than half-a-rope high with simple, easily accessed, natural anchors (trees) or fixed belays (bolts) and a belay position on the ground. Safety management is limited to precautions.

The advanced chapters expand the options and introduce more sophisticated techniques, but assume that the reader has a practical understanding of everything covered in the basic chapters. These chapters are for the climber who wants to be able to go to sites requiring more complex anchoring and belaying systems. Topics covered include: constructing anchors with chocks and cams, belaying from above, and techniques for longer and steeper routes. Safety management systems include basic self-rescue techniques.

This book can be used by instructors, guides and climbing schools as a basis for a single-pitch operations manual, or as a curriculum for teaching toproping to their students.

If you are new to climbing and the basic chapters seem daunting, you have two basic options before utilizing this book: get training from a professional instructor or find a competent mentor. Neither option is as simple as it sounds because competency is hard to quantify.

Just because an individual or institution is in the business of teaching climbing doesn't give you any guarantee regarding the quality of their programs or the expertise of their instructors. And just because someone owns a rack and a rope does not mean he or she will be a safe partner and mentor.

Professional mountain guiding is virtually unregulated in this country—anyone can hang out a shingle or print up a business card and call himself a climbing instructor. The American Mountain Guides Association (AMGA) is the country's first and only organization to promote a uniform, comprehensive, nationwide training and evaluation program for mountain guides. The AMGA has a program that certifies individual guides based on an international standard. The AMGA also accredits climbing schools that pass a brief safety review. You are encouraged to contact them for a list of guides and schools in your area (710 10th St., Ste. 101, Golden, CO 80401, www.climbnet.com/amga 303-271-0984). In addition, when you are considering hiring a guide, get as many references as possible and call them. Don't rely only on the opinion of past clients; they are often not informed enough to know when they have received substandard service. Ask at your local climbing shop and other guides in the area. Find out if the guide or school carries insurance, if they have permits for the areas they are going to take you to, and if they have guide training and first aid standards.

Choosing a mentor is even more difficult. It's like hitch-hiking; neither the driver nor the hitchhiker knows what he's going to get. And unlike areas in Europe where both driver and hitchhiker are licensed, in the US anyone can be your climbing partner. To help you identify a good mentor, here are a few things to look for:

- What is his or her reputation in the climbing community? Ask around, check references.
- Does he or she appear safety-conscious or safety-casual? Confident and cautious, or arrogant?
- Does he or she wear a helmet?
- Does he or she practice fundamental safety procedures such as: using multipoint, equalized anchors with double carabiners; backing up or belaying rappels; double-checking anchors, knots and buckles; using proper climbing signals?
- Is his or her equipment in good repair and is it treated with respect, or does he or she step on the ropes and throw the gear around?

THE TRANSITION FROM GYM TO CLIFF

In the last decade the number of climbing gyms has grown like the national debt. New gyms open regularly across the country and most major cities have at least one. Today it's more likely that a person's first handhold will be made of plastic instead of rock.

At first glance the only difference between climbing in a gym and climbing outside appears to be the medium: rock versus plastic. In both places you'll find ropes, shoes, harnesses, carabiners, belay devices and anchors. In both environments people will be using handholds and footholds to climb up to an anchor and then they'll be lowered back down by the belayer. But first impressions are often inaccurate, and in this case the comparison doesn't hold. The difference is that the indoor environment is primarily experiential—it's valet climbing where everything is set up for you. You can climb in a gym for a long time without learning anything other than how to make moves. Outdoors you are on your own and if you don't have a practical understanding of the basics, you could quickly be in trouble.

One day not too long ago my partner and I were sport climbing at a local crag when two young guys walked up the path and said, "Hello." One of them had a rope and the other was carrying a gym bag. They both looked up at all the bolts and appeared to be bewildered. One of them walked over to where I was belaying. "Excuse me," he said quietly, "but where are the draws?" I answered as politely as I could, "You have to bring your own and lead the routes." "Oh," he said sadly and walked back to his friend. They began talking and a minute or so later they headed back down to their car. Not only did they lack the gear, they obviously lacked any real understanding of what climbing is all about. Even if they had possessed the gear, they probably wouldn't have been capable of climbing safely. They were smart enough to head home.

Even if you can crank really hard moves on plastic, but all your experience has been indoors, focus your attention on the basic systems outlined in this book—and take it slow.

Site Considerations

Deciding where to go toproping involves preparation and a little legwork. There are hundreds—perhaps even thousands—of developed toprope areas in the U.S. And the possibilities are nearly endless when you head into the undeveloped backcountry. Your choices may be well-known to you, or they may be unknown if you are new to outdoor climbing or are visiting an area for the first time. To identify potential destinations try the following:

- Check at the local climbing shop or gym. Ask the people who work there. Post a note on their bulletin board asking for information.
- Consult a guidebook to the area: frequently, toprope sites will be specifically identified and helpful hints provided. (i.e., "Bring long slings for anchors," "Mostly easy routes," "Crowded on Saturdays," etc.)

Once you have a list of potential places to go, several things must be considered:

- The characteristics of the climbing: What type of climbing do you want to do? Crack, face, slab, overhangs, etc.
- The difficulty and selection of routes: Pick areas where you will have a number of appropriately challenging options.
- The logistics: Length of approach and descent, ease of access to anchors (i.e., walk to fixed anchors, lead pitch first, etc.), exposure (i.e., sun/shade, hot/cool), time available to climb (i.e., after work, half-a-day, all day).
- The experience desired: Recreation, climbing technique training, climbing system training (i.e., anchor building, lead practice).
- Safety system requirements: From simple anchors and belays (i.e., short routes, trees for anchors, routes straight up and down), to complex (i.e., longer routes, anchors must be constructed, directionals needed, routes overhang).

When deciding where to go and what to do, always consider your technical proficiency first. Estimate your abilities conservatively and proceed slowly. Some of you may already be competent enough to set up topropes anywhere and meet every technical challenge, while others of you may need to initially limit yourselves to areas requiring only the simplest anchors and belays.

- *Check the local climbing shop or gym for recommendations. Ask the people who work there. Or post a note on the bulletin board asking for beta.*
- *Consult a guidebook to the area. Many books identify TRs and give helpful hints such as "Bring long slings for anchors."*

Once You Hone In On A Destination, Consider:

- *The characteristics of the climbing. What type of climbing do you want to do? Crack, face, slab, overhanging?*
- *The difficulty and selection of routes. (Pick a spot with a number of appropriately challenging options.*
- *The length of approach and descent, ease of access to anchors, exposure, time available to climb.*
- *The desired experience. Is this for recreation? Climbing technique training? Or for anchor building and lead practice?*
- *The safety system requirements. Are simple anchor and belay set-ups sufficient? Or must complex anchors with directionals be constructed?*

RISK

It's easy when you go climbing to get lost in the excitement of the experience itself: the challenge of being up there making moves and getting to the top! But look in the front of most books or magazines that cover climbing and you will see a disclaimer stating in some fashion that "climbing is dangerous."

Everyone knows that climbing is dangerous, but minimizing the dangers requires an understanding of risk. A buzz-phrase often heard these days is "Risk Management" and while it sounds neat and impressive, it really isn't accurate. "Management" indicates control, but risk is often beyond the climber's ability to control. For instance, exactly how would you "manage" lightning? Risk can be minimized, but not always managed.

Risk has two sources and they must both be dealt with if risk is to be minimized. The first source of risk is environmental and includes such things as gravity, weather, rockfall, cliff edges, etc. These types of risks are best defined as "objective hazards." Accidents arising from objective hazards are often attributed to "an act of God." They defy "management" but they can be assessed and reduced.

The second source of risk is brought to the crag by the climbers themselves. It is risk that raises its ugly head when climbers try to climb routes requiring technical skills they do not possess; when they get sloppy; or when they are unaware of hazards. Accidents arising from climber-generated risks are defined as "subjective hazards" and are attributed to "pilot error." Unlike most objective hazards, subjective hazards can usually be controlled through "safety management."

So there you have it. The vague concept of "Risk Management" is replaced with "Hazard Assessment" and "Safety Management." Potential risks, both environmental and climber-generated, are assessed and then steps are taken to ensure they are minimized.

Risk comes in all shapes and sizes and it is helpful to look at it on two levels: macro—the big picture, and micro—the little things. On the macro level such things as the weather, rockfall hazard, and length and difficulty of the approach need to be considered, while on the micro level it's important to check knots and anchors, keep excess slack out of the system, watch for poison ivy at the base of the route, etc. Paying attention to one at the expense of the other can increase risk; a climber distracted by an impending storm may forget to double-back the harness buckle, or a climber absorbed with trying a favorite route may race to set up and get to the crux and leave his or her helmet in the pack. Danger is minimized when all risk is accounted for and a comprehensive safety management system is devised. This doesn't necessarily need to be formal or complicated. Often, the appropriate safety management systems involve simply taking the basic precautions and staying alert.

The following is an introduction to basic hazard assessment and reduction. Specific safety management systems will be discussed in detail in later chapters.

Hazard reduction involves three steps:
1. Identify and analyze potential hazards.
2. Avoid hazards whenever possible.
3. Minimize exposure if hazards cannot be avoided entirely.

APPROACHES AND DESCENTS

Just getting to a climb can be challenging and occasionally dangerous. One day I was sitting in the parking lot at the base of Cathedral Ledge in New Hampshire looking for someone to go climbing with when out of the woods stumbled my best friend Dave. While I walked over he opened the sliding door on his ancient VW van and sat down dejectedly. "Hey Dave, wanna do a route?" He looked at me sadly. "Can't," he said sadly, "I sprained my ankle." I sat down next to him and watched him gently remove his Teva™ from his swollen foot. "How'd you do that?" I asked. "Walking up to *Funhouse* (a great, two-pitch 5.7). I slipped in the talus and fell in a hole."

Now, sandals may be appropriate for walking to some places—the Bastille in Eldorado Canyon, perhaps, because it's on the road—but they're not recommended in talus. This example illustrates that sometimes it can be the simplest things that trip you up and spoil a day of climbing.

The length and difficulty of the approach and descent should always be taken into account when planning a climb.

As you will see by the definitions below, my friend Dave turned Class II terrain into Class III by wearing sandals. Terrain difficulty is rated on a six class scale:

Class I Walking, no use of hands, (most trails, open, gently sloping terrain).

Class II Rough walking, little use of hands (steep trails and slopes, easy scree and talus, proper footwear recommended).

Class III Scrambling, hands used for balance and occasionally for progress, exposure sufficient that a slip could cause injury, novices may require a belay (steep, large talus, blocky mountain ridges, or short, low-angled slabs).

Class IV Climbing where footholds are chosen individually and handholds are necessary for progress, exposure sufficient that a slip could turn into a fatal fall, anchors needed as well as occasional intermediate protection, climbers usually move together without individual belays (steeper mountain ridges or approach slabs).

Class V Belayed free climbing where specialized equipment is needed, anchors and frequent intermediate protection are used, climbers ascend with individual belays using hands and feet only for progress (in the American rock climbing rating system all free climbs are rated Class V and the class is further broken down into sub-ratings from 5.0 to 5.14. The ratings 5.10-5.14 are additionally broken down into a,b,c,d).

Class VI Belayed aid climbing where progress can no longer be made using footholds and handholds, sophisticated and often specialized equipment is placed and pulled on by the climber to make progress. (Most big wall routes involve aid climbing and the class is broken into ratings of A1 to A6, the higher the number the less secure the gear placements are and the greater the likelihood of a long and potentially dangerous fall.)

Approaches and descents to toprope sites are rarely harder than Class III, but you should carefully analyze each one to determine what precautions to take. There are times when extra safety is needed: on wet slabs for instance, or if a member of the party is nervous. When in doubt, belay, even if the terrain wouldn't usually warrant it. In too many accident reports you find the phrase "unroped fall on easy ground."

Dangerous edges can be encountered anytime, even on the approach to a climb. A smart climber will carry his helmet on his head at the first sign of risk.

ON-SITE HAZARD ASSESSMENT

Assessing hazards on approaches and descents is just part of the job. While at the climbing site there are a number of potential hazards not directly related to the climbing itself that must be dealt with.

Edges

Any edge, whether at the top or bottom, poses potential hazards. An edge is any change in terrain abrupt enough and high enough to be dangerous if you fall off it, or if something falls off it onto you. While most would consider both the top and bottom of a cliff to be edges worthy of caution, much smaller edges can also be dangerous. A climbing route that starts off a ten-foot block; a trail that crosses the top of a short, wet slab; a short wall that must be traversed to reach an anchor—all are potentially dangerous edges that deserve assessment. Even something as common as crossing a slope of large talus is nothing more than climbing over a series of small, dangerous edges. The next time you're in a talus field, stop for a moment and think how it would be to stumble and fall head first off of any of the boulders. You may decide that wearing your helmet on the approach is a good idea. Hazard reduction in situations like these is often as simple as alerting others and then detouring.

I have seen the tragic consequences of climbers ignoring seemingly insignificant edges. On two occasions while I was living in New Hampshire, climbers were killed in ten-foot falls on easy ground. One was killed while scrambling up a short slab to set up a toprope, and another died after he tripped in talus and landed on his head. But one experience in particular has reinforced my respect for edges.

It was in 1979 at the top of a cliff in the Adirondacks. My partner Mark and I had just completed the ascent of what we hoped was a new route. Mark put all the gear in his pack, I threw the coiled rope over my shoulder, and we began to walk down. We were full of excitement from our successful climb and not paying particular attention as we walked west along the top edge of the cliff. After just a hundred feet or so I came to a little bush and took one step to the left onto a slab. It was wet and mossy and I instantly lost my footing, landed on my butt, slid ten feet down the slab and off the top of the cliff. The cliff is 150 feet high, nearly vertical, and sits on top of nasty talus. After I slid out of sight Mark didn't even bother to call my name. He just started walking slowly down. He was so certain that I had been killed that he was going to go right to the car and drive to town to get help. A moment later I shouted his name and he nearly fainted. There was one ledge on this particular cliff. It's about three feet wide, ten feet long, and I landed on one end of it. I had free-fallen onto the ledge feet first—the impact severely damaging both ankles— teetered for a moment, and then fell left onto the ledge. Had I taken one more step, or fallen to the right instead of the left, I would have gone the full distance into the talus. I know God had his hand on me that day, nudging me onto the ledge. By the way, the name of the cliff is Pitchoff and the climb I fell off of is called *Pete's Farewell*. OK, it's funny now.

Falling Objects

A fall from an edge is only one hazard; things can also fall off of them and hit you. One of the most dangerous occurrences, and most common, is rockfall. Some rockfall is the natural sloughing off of loose rock that occurs to a greater or lesser extent on all cliffs. This hazard is usually well known and consulting a guidebook or local climbers will help you identify cliffs requiring extra caution.

Without specific knowledge about a cliff, on-site assessment should be one of the climber's first tasks. Natural rockfall is obviously most common on cliffs that are heavily fractured or have sections of decomposing rock. At some cliffs the climbing itself may be on solid rock but rockfall danger is still very high. There is a wonderful sport crag in Clear Creek Canyon in Colorado called the Little Eiger. There are a dozen or more routes here, all but one confined to the lower 75 feet of the crag on vertical, very solid gneiss. From the base of the routes the belayer can only see to the anchors; the rest of the cliff leans back out of sight. I have rarely seen climbers wear helmets here, and for the most part they seem unaware of the danger lurking above. One glance from the road, however, reveals a 400-foot pile of decomposing, fractured rock looming above the sport routes—a more serious danger could not exist.

In addition to spontaneous, natural rockfall there is also human-generated rockfall. The source can be from climbers in your own party, other climbers above, or from hikers on a trail above the crag.

Several years ago I experienced an episode that drove home the need for taking precautions against rockfall. I was at the top of Square Ledge in Pinkham Notch, New Hampshire, on a perfect summer day. I was belaying one client up a 5.4 route while my two other clients stood about fifteen feet apart at the bottom of the cliff and watched. Another guide named Dave was next to me with his clients. About fifty feet up my client stepped on a foothold and a chunk about the size of a toaster broke off. Dave and I both yelled, "Rock!" as loud as we could. We watched the rock spin in the air and hit the cliff halfway to the ground. It split in two and then each piece spiraled in and hit a client. It was like making the 7-10 split in bowling, only much harder. Each client was struck in the head, one directly, the other with a glancing blow. Fortunately they were both were wearing helmets and there were no injuries.

Another hazard is equipment dropped by climbers. While nothing a climber can drop is going to be as injurious as a big rock, objects like figure eight devices and locking carabiners can do serious damage when they fall.

One day when I was preparing to climb a route on Whitehorse Ledge in New Hampshire, a humorous incident occurred which involved some falling gear. Fellow guide Marc Chauvin and I were both at the *Launch Pad*, about a hundred feet off the ground with our clients. From somewhere in the gray ocean above we began to hear shouting, faint at first, but then the word "Rock!" came through clearly. Then we heard something off to the north, pinging down the granite over near *Beginner's Route*. We both listened for a moment while our clients sat anxiously, trying to stay small under their helmets. "Belay plate," I finally commented assuredly. Marc cocked his head and listened intently for another moment. The object pinged again, taking a high bounce before crashing into the woods. Marc nodded, "Yup, with no spring," he said confidently. Our clients were very impressed. Neither Marc nor I had any idea what the thing was.

This anecdote does raise the question of what to do with dropped gear. My best source recommends not using gear that has experienced a bad impact. Now just what is a bad impact? A full pitch into talus is bad. Dropped onto the ground while racking your gear is not bad. In between? Well, it's going to have to be your call. If you think a piece of gear may have hit hard, don't trust your life to it.

To minimize the danger of being hit by falling objects:
• Identify hazard potential by consulting guidebooks and local climbers.
• Assess the conditions at the site.
• Avoid hazards by positioning your party in the safest locations.
• Minimize exposure by taking basic precautions (i.e., wear your helmet).

Whenever a climber knows that an object is falling, (whether he or she sees a rock fall or drops a carabiner), the proper response is to shout, "Rock!" several times as loud as possible. Don't worry about identifying the object: "See large rock, get out of the way." A hundred yards away it may sound like: "Need large chock for the belay," and your warning may go unheeded. Once, while climbing at Ragged Mountain, I heard someone yell, "Lunch!" several times. A brown paper bag hit the ground and a thermos rolled out. Great presence of mind but, "Rock!" would still have been a more appropriate warning.

If you hear someone yell, "Rock!" there are three things you should do (they sound obvious but the opposite is instinctive and you'll have to train yourself):
1. Look straight ahead, not up or down.
2. Stand up and keep your hands at your sides.
3. Stay put. If you run you're more likely to trip and hurt yourself, and besides, "Over there" is rarely better than where you are. The only exception would be if several easy steps took you to substantial cover.

Other Hazards

Always check the weather forecast for thunderstorms or high wind warnings and act accordingly. Bring rain gear, sun screen, or bug repellent as conditions warrant. Be cautious crossing streams. Crowded sites can be hazardous, especially if there is loose rock. Include alternate sites and routes in your plans.

ENVIRONMENTAL CONCERNS

The increase in popularity of outdoor recreation has put a tremendous strain on the environment. By observing a few basic principles you can help minimize your damage to the environment.

Trails

- Stay on established trails.
- Walk in single file—braided trails caused by walking abreast increase erosion.
- Don't cut switchbacks.

Trees

- Never toprope by running the rope directly around a tree—doing this repeatedly can wear through the bark and kill the tree—not to mention dangerously abrade the rope!
- Trees growing on cliffs are often shallow-rooted, and repeated use can compact and erode what little soil there is—assess stability before trusting any tree and back it up if there is any question. If you have the expertise, consider constructing a gear anchor instead of using a tree.

Waste

- Pack out more than you pack in. Tape, old slings, aluminum cans—they're light, don't leave them behind.
- Dispose of human waste properly. Take the time to get well away from the climbing area. Dig a hole, bury waste, and pack out paper.
- Don't build fires.

ETHICS

Sharing Routes

- Be nice.
- Don't monopolize routes.
- Respect other climbers' rights to use a route for as long as they need, and have alternative route options in mind.
- Be very cautious about using anyone else's toprope—regardless of how friendly the offer—unless you are absolutely certain the anchor is solid. One day my partner and I were at a popular toprope crag, rounding out the day with a couple of quick pitches. Some folks next to us had a rope set up on a popular 5.9 crack and we naturally struck up a conversation. After the second guy had finished they offered us their toprope to do the route. My friend Geoff asked what their anchor was, and one of them said, "We've got it through a sling." Since Geoff and I both knew that there was a tree above the route, we assumed that they had slung the tree and were running the rope through double biners. We thanked them for their generosity, Geoff tied in, and I belayed him up the route. Fortunately he never fell, because when he got to the top he found that they had indeed run the rope "through a sling." Just a sling. Both of them had already lowered off it and it was melted halfway through. Geoff dropped their rope to them, untied their

anchor and walked down carrying the sling. When they saw it they were horrified. We were irresponsible for not checking more thoroughly.
- Don't sandbag (grossly understate the difficulty of a route), especially with strangers. It could put them in danger.

Assisting Others

- If you see people who appear to be climbing dangerously, intervention may be appropriate—use your best judgment. If it is life-threatening, do something. One day I was topping out on a one-pitch 5.6 at Jockey Cap, a small crag in western

ACCESS: If signs are posted at climbing areas, read them. Respect closures and other site specific rules.

Maine, when I looked over and saw a tragedy in the making. Another climber was standing at the top of the crag belaying his partner up a 5.8 flake. The climber was struggling and yelling, "Tension!" The belayer was leaning off his belay anchor, which appeared to be just a single piece under a flake. I yelled, "Off belay!" to my client, ran over and peered under the flake. I found a single, poorly placed cam just under the lip of an obviously fragile flake. "Watch me!" yelled the struggling climber. I grabbed some slack from the belayer's rope, ran twenty feet to a tree, flipped a sling around it, pulled the rope tight and clipped the belayer in. "Hey, what do you think you're doing?" the guy yelled at me. His partner made the last few moves and then the belayer stomped over and got right in my face. He was fuming. "What the *&?@! do you think you're doing messing with my anchor?" "Anchor?" I said angrily. I walked over, grabbed the sling on his cam, and yanked hard on it twice. The edge of the flake busted and the cam flew out. "Here's your 'anchor,'" I said with disgust, dangling the cam in front of him. The climber turned white. The belayer said nothing, grabbed the sling, and walked away.
- If an accident occurs, do everything you can to assist and comfort. Let the most medically qualified person take charge, and then do what they say.

Access

- Find out who owns the land you plan to climb on. Consult the guidebook or ask locals. ALWAYS ASK PERMISSION TO CLIMB ON PRIVATE LAND.
- Abide by all the rules. Be courteous.
- Respect closures. These are often only temporary, as in the case of nesting raptors—even if it means that you must skip a terrific area while on a road trip.
- Get involved in your local climbing community and work to solve access problems.
- Join the Access Fund if you want to become more actively involved in solving climbing access problems.

Everything you need—and more.

S. Peter Lewis

Basic Equipment

There is a tremendous quantity of high-tech climbing gear available today. Climbers interested in toproping only need the basics. Fundamental, simple equipment in many instances is more versatile and less expensive than the flashy stuff. So just buy the essentials—rope, slings, harness, carabiners, belay/rappel device, helmet, shoes—and use the savings to buy gas on your next climbing trip.

ROPE

Modern nylon climbing ropes have been around since World War II. Before then, natural fiber ropes were used by climbers, but the ropes' strength characteristics were so poor they were capable of holding only the shortest of falls. The invention of nylon gave climbers a material that was capable of absorbing the shock forces generated in a long climbing fall without breaking.

Originally, nylon climbing ropes were woven in three strands, were relatively stiff and hard to handle, and stretched a lot when under a body-weight load (static elongation), which made them tricky to manage when rappelling. By the 1970s *kernmantle* (core and sheath) construction had arrived, giving ropes much better handling characteristics, lower static elongation and greater abrasion resistance. Though made of the same material, the core and sheath are woven differently because they are required to perform different functions. The core, which accounts for about 85 per cent of the rope's strength, is made up of thin, full-length, continuous fibers that are twisted into bundles. The sheath accounts for the remainder of the rope's strength and is woven in a dense, cross-hatch pattern providing the abrasion resistance required to protect the core. With only subtle variations, climbing ropes are constructed the same today as they were 40 years ago.

There are two basic rope types used in outdoor recreation: *dynamic* ropes, which stretch significantly under a load; and *static* ropes, which stretch very little when loaded. Climbers use dynamic ropes because they need a rope capable of absorbing the forces generated in a fall. Spelunkers, or those who exclusively rappel, use static ropes because the lack of stretch makes these ropes more manageable under body-weight loads. Static ropes cannot be used as lead ropes because their lack of stretch would transmit extremely high forces to the equipment and the climber and could cause failure and serious injury.

Rope: Those Confusing Numbers

Check out the tag on a new rope and you'll see weird terms and strange numbers. What do they mean? Frequently misunderstood, the data is easy to understand. Let's shatter a couple of myths:

MYTH: How much a rope can hold—it's tensile strength—is most important.
FACT: Under normal climbing conditions, undamaged ropes don't fail because their tensile strength isn't high enough—a falling climber cannot generate enough force to exceed the tensile strength.

MYTH: A climbing rope can only hold the number of falls it's rated for.
FACT: The rating is for the number of laboratory test falls that the rope held before failure. No climber can duplicate the severity of the test fall under normal climbing conditions. Ropes can hold more falls than they are rated for before they should be retired.

A rope is a marvelously engineered tool. By utilizing elasticity in the materials and design, manufactures are able to produce ropes that protect climbers from injury by cushioning their falls. Wrapping the core with an abrasion resistant sheath gives the rope great durability.

A rope's strength lies in it's ability to absorb force. A falling climber can generate a force greatly in excess of their weight (anyone who has had a child jump on them unexpectedly know this). If a rope was as inelastic as a steel cable the force of even a short fall would cause severe injury. Fortunately, nylon works better than steel. Of all the numbers that a new rope brings with it, three need to be understood by the climber in order to help them purchase the right rope for their needs.

Static elongation—the amount a rope will stretch under a body-weight load, expressed as a percentage of its length. UIAA (Union Internationale Des Associations Alpines) is the international testing agency for climbing equipment. They use an 80kg (176 lb.) weight in most of their rope tests. This represents the weight of the average climber plus their gear. In this test, the higher the stretch the better job a rope does of cushioning a fall—but at the cost of increased distance. For toproping, lower static elongation is preferred—less stretch means shorter falls under body-weight and less chance of injury.

Maximum impact force—expressed in units of force such as daN (decanewtons) or kN (kilonewtons)—is the maximum force that can be exerted by the climber on the rope. When a falling climber stops and all the stretch is out of the rope, the force remaining is the impact force. The UIAA uses the most severe fall possible to determine a rope's maximum impact force. The maximum allowable impact force is 2,680 lbs.—this is the most force a climber can momentarily withstand without injury. With a tensile strength normally over 5,000 lbs, it's clear that no falling climber can "break" an undamaged rope. The higher the impact force, the less elastic rope is in a lead-fall situation—not of great concern to the toprope climber. Don't worry too much about this.

UIAA test falls held—the number of test falls held before failure. This is perhaps the most misunderstood strength characteristic. In the most severe test situation possible the 80 kg. weight is dropped repeatedly, stressing the same point over and over again with no chance for the rope to recover much of its elasticity. With each succeeding fall the rope has less ability to stretch, the impact force rises, and eventually exceeds the tensile strength. The test fall cannot be duplicated under normal climbing conditions and an climber who repeatedly takes sever falls without rest should consider counseling. A climbing rope is capable of catching more than the rated number of lead falls and hundreds of top rope falls. The more falls a rope is rated for, the more durable it is.

For toproping, durability is by far the most important factor. A wise choice would be an 11mm rope with a highly abrasive sheath, low static elongation, relatively high impact force, and rated to hold lots of falls. Leave the skinny, stretchy ropes to the sport climbers who want to save every once of weight on that 5.14 redpoint attempt.

A dynamic rope acts like the shock absorber on your car. When loaded with body-weight, or slightly more (like those encountered rappelling), or during most toprope falls the rope stretches very little, giving the user better control. But when called upon to hold a high force like that generated in a lead fall, the rope can stretch up to half its length to dampen the load. This limits the force on the equipment, and more importantly on the climber, to levels that can be sustained without damage. This characteristic of being nearly static when under a normal working load (body-weight) and very dynamic under a shock-load gives modern ropes superb handling characteristics. Your car's shocks do the same, dampening very little on smooth roads, but absorbing huge shocks when you're out four-wheeling. If ropes were always stretchy they would handle like a 1965 station wagon with original shocks that bounces, drifts and weaves across both lanes.

Modern climbing ropes come in a variety of different lengths and diameter configurations. Many are highly specialized and not applicable to toproping. For toproping a rope that is 11 millimeters in diameter and 50 meters (165 feet) long is all you need. Thinner ropes are less durable and longer ropes are harder to manage. And don't be concerned with the extra weight of a chunky 11mm rope—most of the time you won't be carrying it very far.

A rope is one of the most expensive items you'll buy, but when you consider what you are asking it to do, it really is very inexpensive life insurance. Don't buy used ropes, no matter how careful the owner was or how certain he or she is that the rope is still serviceable: you will never know for sure.

I once learned a lesson about chemical damage when I was living in Maine. I was working in my garden one day in June and the black flies were so thick that it was hard to see across the back field. As a defense against these hideous carnivores I had smothered myself with a non-prescription bug repellent composed of 100% Deet™. It was nasty stuff, but like most people in northern New England I had decided it was worth it. Ears are particularly susceptible so I had lathered it on them extra thick. A little while later my wife called from the house and told me I had a phone call. I went in and took the call and when I hung the phone back up on the wall, strands of liquid plastic sagged between my ear and the receiver like hot taffy. I never touched a rope again without making sure my hands were free of bug repellent.

Battery acid is another danger that must be avoided. Even a little residue on a pair of jumper cables in the trunk of a car can destroy a rope. The worst part is that the damage to ropes is invisible; the rope is weakened without any change in its appearance. Another auto hazard is heat. The back seat of a black car on a sunny June day can raise the temperature enough to cook an egg. It will cook your rope too, so keep it cool.

Use a rope bag at the crags. When the rope gets dirty, wash it in a bathtub with very mild detergent (commercial rope cleaning solutions are also available) and air dry.

Keeping your rope clean will add to its useful life span.

If you do all these things the rope will last a reasonable amount of time. Exactly how long is hard to say. Nylon breaks down naturally over time and ropes stored under perfect conditions for 20 years have failed under startlingly low loads. With the best of care and weekend toprope use you can expect your rope to last three-to-five seasons. When to retire a rope is based on several factors: age, sheath wear, number of high-force lead falls (not toprope falls), core damage (mushy spots can be cut out if they are near the end). Perhaps the most important consideration is when you lose faith in it—for whatever reason. A retired rope is useful for many things but it should not be used again to support people. Dip the ends in black paint and never bring it out of retirement.

WEBBING

Webbing is essential in making connections between the rope and other equipment in the climbing system. Slings made of webbing are used for building anchors, connecting carabiners to the rope, and many other things.

Webbing is made of several materials and comes in many dimensions. The most common material is a nylon product called Perlon™ although another material called Spectra™ is also common. Though the materials have different properties they will be considered identical here. For toproping, only two widths, ⁹⁄₁₆-inch and 1-inch, are needed. The 1-inch webbing is used primarily in building anchoring systems where its greater width provides extra abrasion resistance. The ⁹⁄₁₆-inch webbing is the most versatile, being applicable for nearly every climbing task where a sling is needed.

Both widths are available by the foot at climbing shops. Tied in a loop with a water knot, (see Basic Knots, p 29) this allows the climber to make slings to any length needed. The ⁹⁄₁₆-inch webbing is also available pre-sewn in convenient lengths from 4 inches to 6 feet and is used for anything from making quickdraws (two carabiners connected by a short sling for use on protection placements) to building anchors. Sewn slings have a higher breaking strength than knotted slings, but knotted slings are absolutely strong enough, and they're more versatile—they can be untied and wrapped around a large tree, for instance. A selection of both is recommended.

HARNESSES

Harnesses are fairly new to climbing. Twenty-five years ago climbers just wrapped two-inch webbing around their waists. Yes, it's as uncomfortable as it sounds, and dangerous. These original *swami belts* put all of a climber's weight on his or her waist. While hanging in it the swami would slowly creep upward to the climber's rib cage, making it difficult to breath—in rare cases causing suffocation. Modern harnesses use leg loops, transmitting most of the climber's weight to the back of the legs. Though it can be uncomfortable to hang this way for a long time, at least it's not life-threatening.

Harnesses come in an amazing variety of shapes and sizes, designed to fit every purpose and body type. They form part of the vital link between the climber and the rope. Their basic job is to protect the climber from harm when a fall occurs.

There are four basic harness styles: the first combines a waist belt with a pair of permanently sewn leg loops. This "swami/leg loop" style is very comfortable to hang in, and can be made very lightweight. But they do not fit a range of sizes and therefore one harness of this type cannot be used by the same person in summer and winter and will not fit properly on anyone who has a different build than the owner. This is the most common style for people who exclusively rock climb.

The second style, referred to as an *alpine harness*, has a conventional waist belt but no pre-formed leg loops. The leg loops are formed by connecting a loop of webbing to the waist belt with a buckle at each hip. The advantages of an alpine-style harness are that they can be put on over clothing, skis, crampons, etc.—hence the name "alpine," and adjust to fit properly whether wearing shorts or full expedition clothing. A disadvantage to these harnesses is that they are not nearly as comfortable to hang in as those with fixed leg loops.

The third style, the *adjustable harness,* is like the swami/leg loop style but adds a buckle to each leg loop making the entire harness adjustable. Adjustable harnesses are bulkier and heavier than the other styles.

The fourth style, called a "full body harness," combines any of the above three with a chest harness. Body harnesses can be purchased complete, or an improvised chest harness can be combined with any of the first three styles. A full body harness is recommended for small children.

Tip #5: A Harness Must Be...

- Sized properly: leg loops should be snug, and the ends of the padded waist belt should nearly meet when pulled across the waist.

- Snug and above the hips: if after buckling the harness it is possible to pull it down over the hips, it's too loose! If you fell upside-down you could slip out of the harness and die. It is especially important to size and fit a harness correctly on thin people, fat people, and most children.

- Buckled correctly: a harness can be sized and fitted correctly, but if the buckle is not properly fastened the harness will not hold you. Harnesses come with multi-pass buckles wherein the webbing passes at least twice through the buckle, trapping the webbing on the second pass. If the second pass is not made, the buckle will fail and you could die.

Three basic 'biner styles (L to R): Petzl Locker, Black Diamond Light D and Climb High oval. Modified Ds, bent gates and live/hot wires are simply variations on these themes.

CARABINERS

Carabiners are a climber's most important piece of hardware. Give an expert some carabiners and he can belay, rappel, and perform many other tasks. Carabiners are aluminum snap links used to connect all pieces of a climbing system together.

Carabiners get their strength from their design. When loaded along their long axis with the gate shut they are extremely strong. If cross-loaded against the gate, loaded with their gate open, or loaded over an edge, they may fail. Another loading situation that compromises the strength is *tri-axial* loading. This occurs when a carabiner has three things clipped to it, all loading in different directions. Avoid loading a carabiner this way. Another thing to avoid is chaining carabiners together to lengthen a connection in the system. If subjected to a twisting motion they can unclip themselves.

One day I was at the top of a five-pitch route on Cathedral Ledge with a client. Next to us was another local guide named Brad who was belaying his clients up the last pitch. I was talking about the possible dangers of linking carabiners together into a chain and decided to illustrate the lesson. I took three carabiners and clipped them together forming a chain. I held them up in front of me, said something like, "If you twist these…" Then I paused dramatically and gave the whole chain a vigorous twist. The middle carabiner snapped free, hung in front of us for a moment and then fell five hundred feet to the ground. Brad politely shouted "Rock!" while I stood there with a dumb look on my face, holding the two carabiners. Brad smiled weakly and said, "Nice illustration." (The company I was guiding for at the time, Eastern Mountain Sports Climbing School, had a gear replacement policy. I didn't even ask.)

Four types of carabiners will be briefly described, although only two, *ovals* and *locking* carabiners, are needed for toproping.

Oval Carabiner

This has been the standard carabiner design for decades. It does everything well and some things superbly. Its symmetrical design centers the load thus placing equal weight on each side of the long axis. Because of this, oval carabiners are not as strong as some other designs, but they are plenty strong enough. They are well-suited for use as the *master point* in a belay anchor. (See Chapter 4.)

D Carabiner

This design uses an asymmetrical shape to direct more of the load on the spine of the carabiner. Because of this, D carabiners can be made lighter that ovals and still retain adequate strength. They are suitable for most climbing uses.

Bent Gate Carabiner

These use a bend in the gate to make clipping it easier. They are highly specialized and can be dangerous if used incorrectly. They should not be used for toproping.

Locking Carabiner

In addition to standard oval carabiners you will want to carry one or two *locking* carabiners. Locking carabiners all have a mechanism that when activated makes it extremely difficult to unlock the gate. They provide added security when a pair is used on a belay anchor. With proper monitoring they can be used singly for belaying and rappelling.

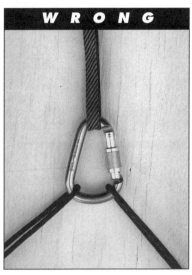

Like non-locking carabiners, lockers come in many shapes and sizes. There are oval lockers, Ds, and even funky twisted 3-D lockers. One specialty design is an oval with an extra-large radius at the end opposite the gate hinge and is called an HMS carabiner. It is the only kind suitable for use with a *Munter Hitch*. (See Belay and Rappel Devices, Chapter 3.) Locking carabiners are typically larger than regular carabiners because they are often required to hold several things at once.

There are two basic styles of locking mechanisms: screwgates and twist-locks. A screwgate locker has a threaded sleeve that is spun over one end of the gate. Those with sleeves located on the hinged end are less secure because of the mechanical advantage caused by the gate acting as a lever. Screwgate carabiners are locked and unlocked manually. Twist-lock carabiners have

Tri-axial loading places dangerous stresses on a carabiner and should always be avoided.

a spring-loaded ring that usually keys around a pin and must be slid as well as spun to activate. The simpler designs remain locked until the user twists them open. They then return to their locked position when released. Others have more complex mechanisms that allow them to be kept in either the locked or open positions. Both screwgates and twist-locks provide excellent security, but neither is foolproof. They must be used appropriately and carefully monitored.

There are many other carabiners on the market, some filling specialized needs, like *ultralight* carabiners, which can significantly reduce the weight of a large rack on big walls or alpine routes. Others have wire gates or huge gate openings or gates that are held open and trip shut when the rope is dropped into them. All these carabiners have their uses, but for toproping, none of them offers any advantages over standard ovals—and in some cases their use can compromise safety.

The three basic styles of
belay and rappel devices:
plate, tube and figure 8.

Wild Country Variable
Controller

Black Diamond ATC

Black Diamond Super 8

BELAY AND RAPPEL DEVICES

Belay and rappel devices come in various shapes. They give the climber control of a loaded rope by creating a manageable amount of friction when the rope is threaded through them. They accomplish this by bending the rope and created drag. They are an indispensable part of the toproper's equipment, but again the best advice is to stick to the simplest designs, these tend to be the most versatile and the easiest to use.

There are three basic types of belay and rappel devices:

Plate

This is a simple aluminum disc with a slot (or slots) in it (sometimes called a *stitch* plate.) It can be used for either belaying or rappelling. To use, a *bight* (or loop), of rope is passed through the slot and clipped to a carabiner. The sharp bend creates friction that can be varied from nearly free-running when the strands are held parallel, to locked up when the strands are pulled in opposition. Plates work better for belaying than rappelling. Those with single slots can only belay or rappel a single strand of rope.

Tube

This operates exactly like a plate, but its length allows the climber to control the friction more precisely and smoothly. They work better than plates for rappelling (plus, all tubes can accommodate two strands). With both plates and tubes a second carabiner can be clipped to the bight of rope for smoother operation.

Figure Eight Device

This has been the standard rappel device for decades. It forms a *figure eight,* with one small and one large hole. To rappel, a bight of rope is passed through the large hole, then passed around the small hole, riding in the hollow between the two. The small hole is then clipped to the harness with a locking carabiner. Figure eight devices offer smooth, precise control when rappelling. They are bulkier, however, and tend to twist the rope more than plates or tubes.

Figure eight devices can also be used for belaying by utilizing the smaller hole as a belay plate. Do not belay in the rappel configuration because it doesn't produce enough friction and can be dangerous, as the following will illustrate:

"A climber was leading...failed to make it through the crux, thus falling. (The belayer) was unable to stop the rope from feeding through his figure eight device, thus sustaining injuries to his hand." *Accidents in North American Mountaineering,* 1995, page 52.

In recent years, using a figure eight device in the *sport belay* mode has become fashionable. It is the same as the rappel configuration, except that the bight never passes around the small hole—it is simply clipped into the carabiner after passing through the large hole. This method produces almost no friction, and is appropriate only in certain low-force situations. Serious accidents will result when it is used inappropriately. Do not use the sport belay!

A serious drawback to using the figure eight device, even in the plate mode, is its lack of a keeper cord. Both plates and tubes come with fixed keeper cords and they perform the vital function of keeping the device within reach of the belayer. Without a keeper cord, when belaying from above, it is possible for the belayer to drop the device and have it slide down the rope out of reach. When this happens there is no longer any belay and I know of at least one accident where a broken back resulted. Because figure eight devices don't have keeper cords it is easy to forget them and risk losing the belay. To attach a keeper to a figure eight device, *girth hitch* (described in the Knots section) a two-foot sling to the large hole and clip it to your harness.

HELMETS

Helmets are without a doubt the simplest, easiest way to protect the climber from injury—they are the seat belts of mountaineering. They protect the climber from falling rocks and from impact resulting from a fall. They are made of plastic, fiberglass, or composite materials, and in recent years new designs have increased comfort and security while decreasing weight.

They are a critical piece of equipment and climbing without wearing a helmet is stupid. Two anecdotes will help reinforce how essential they are:

One day, a pitch below the top of Cathedral Ledge, I heard sirens. I climbed to the summit with my clients and walked over to where another guide was peering over the edge. I could tell just by his posture that something really bad was happening. I stood next to him and looked over. Five hundred feet below I saw another guide kneeling on the ground over a climber. I recognized his helmet. "What's Marc doing?" I asked. There was a long pause then Jeff turned and looked at me. "CPR," he said quietly. I don't think either of us could have felt more helpless. Marc told us later that most of the dead climber's gear was brand new, except for his helmet— he didn't have one. He'd fallen leading, caught his leg on the rope, flipped over, and hit his head. He was forty feet off the ground.

In another scenario that topropers may find themselves in, an experienced climber lost control during a slightly diagonalling rappel, and swung and hit his head (swinging falls can also happen while climbing). Blood started dripping down the rock and he began fading in and out of consciousness. His partners watched in horror, their eyes fixed on his brake hand. He had no rappel backup and there was no knot in the end of the rope. No one could reach him. He lived, but although the impact of the swing hadn't killed him, the hundred-foot ride to the ground surely would have.

"But helmets don't look cool!" Does it look cool to have a big hole in your head? I guarantee that once you get in the habit you won't even notice you are wearing it. "But they're hot and itchy." That will sound like a very stupid excuse at your funeral.

Wear your helmet. Put it on early, take it off late. Have your belayer wear one. Have everyone on the ground wear one.

SHOES

When I began climbing there were just a couple of brands available, the boxes they came in were more ergonomic, and no one would accuse the manufacturer of using *sticky* rubber. But they were all we had—at least the playing field was level. These days we're spoiled by the variety and functionality of shoes available. There are stiff shoes, soft shoes, slippers, edging shoes, crack shoes, shoes just for limestone pockets, and the list goes on.

But seriously, don't get bogged down looking at every specialized shoe on the market. If you are new to climbing then ask your local clerk to get you one pair of each of the leading manufacturers' all-purpose shoes. Now the trick is to pick the one that fits best. And exactly how should they fit? Are they supposed to be so tight that all the blood is forced out of your foot? No. Snug shoes give more precise control because your foot moves less inside the shoe. But too tight can be as bad as too loose. A properly fitting shoe will conform to the shape of your foot without any gaps and you will feel the front of the shoe with each toe. A little uncomfortable is okay but they shouldn't hurt. Try one size below your street shoe size. Most shoes will stretch a little so get the advice of the store clerk. And don't worry about the rubber, these days it's all sticky.

Several manufacturers make excellent hybrid shoes that can be used for both the approach and the climb. Up until recently I was too chicken to use anything but tight, highly specialized shoes, even on 5.1. I finally got the nerve to try a pair of hybrid shoes and was pleasantly surprised at how well they climbed. These days I don't put on my tight climbing shoes until things get to be 5.8 or so. It's great wearing just one pair of shoes on the approach and the climb. So if you plan to climb just a little and will mostly be on routes under 5.8, these hybrid shoes may be the perfect choice. They should fit snug, but still be comfortable to walk in.

Basic Toprope System

Finally, we've arrived at the nuts and bolts of toproping. We've picked the site, arrived safely, assessed the hazards and taken basic precautions. We are now equipped and ready to go. This chapter will introduce you to the fundamental principles, techniques and tools needed to climb at most toprope sites. It will cover basic knots, anchoring and belaying systems. If you are new to climbing you will find that this chapter provides all the basic information you need to begin a successful climbing career. Even if you already have some experience you would be wise to read this section carefully to ensure that your climbing foundation is a strong one.

The techniques described here assume that the climbing site is straightforward and that the routes are less than half-a-rope-length long. It also assumes that only single-point, natural anchors (trees, for example), or fixed, double-bolt anchors are needed and that they can be accessed easily from above. This chapter describes only the basic belay setup called a *slingshot,* wherein the rope is doubled through an anchor at the cliff's edge and the climber is belayed from the ground. It will describe in detail the fundamental anchoring and belaying techniques that are used not only for toproping but for all climbing. Emergency management will be limited to precautions and no self-rescue techniques will be described. See the advanced chapters for this information.

BASIC KNOTS

Figure Eight Follow Through

This has been the standard tie-in knot for decades. It forms the vital connection between the climber's harness and the rope. It is simple to tie, easy to identify as correct, stays tight, and is strong. Enough rope should be used so that after being tied, threaded through the harness and re-traced, there is about 18 inches left over. This is tied around the standing end of rope using half of a *double fisherman knot* (see p. 30) as a backup. Knot tying is one area where economy is not necessarily desired. Do not tie the figure eight so that only an inch is left hanging out. A short tail like this may creep into the knot during a climb and cause the knot to fall apart.

The figure eight follow through is the standard tie-in knot, combining strength and security. Tied on a bight of rope, it is also used to make anchor attachments.

The above sequence shows how a figure eight follow through knot is achieved—by retracing the initial figure eight knot!

Figure Eight-on-a-Bight

This is almost the same knot as the figure eight. The difference is that it is tied on a bight of rope instead of threaded and then re-traced. It forms a loop that has many uses, the most common being to clip into a belay anchor. A common question is: why not use the figure eight-on-a-bight and clip the loop to a carabiner on your harness to climb? It's fast and easier than re-tracing the figure eight follow-through. The answer is simple: *clipping in instead of tying in is dangerously insecure.* It is possible for the rope to lay across the gate of the carabiner during a climb and if a fall occurs it could unclip itself. Even using locking carabiners is no guarantee—they aren't always locked prior to climbing and they don't always stay locked. Once you get the hang of it, tying in is fast and easy—and when you're spread-eagled on tiny edges and can't let go with your hands, you won't have to worry.

Girth Hitch

This has many uses, the most common being to link slings together or to attach a long sling around a tree for an anchor. When using the girth hitch be careful not to over-torque it. The sling should form a straight line as it passes through the loop. Bending the girth hitch severely back on itself increases the load without adding any security.

Water Knot

This is a simple re-traced overhand knot and is used to join two pieces of webbing. (See picture p.31.) When complete, both strands of webbing should be flat and parallel with no twists and the tail ends should come out on the opposite sides of the knot and be about two inches long. If you use it to tie your own slings be certain that it is as tight as you can get it.(Hang the sling off something, step in it, and bounce.) Because the tail ends have a tendency to creep into the knot, check before each use and re-tie as necessary. To loosen a tight water knot, roll it under your palm against a hard, flat surface.

Double Fisherman

This knot is used to join two ropes; one-half of a double fisherman knot is used to back up the figure eight tie-in knot.

These basic knots and their variations are all that are required in most climbing situations. Many people have climbed for years using just these five knots.

BASIC TOPROPE SYSTEM

The basic toprope anchoring system is called a *slingshot belay* and consists of an anchor at the top of a route with the rope running through it. Initially both rope ends are on the ground, the climber tied into one end and the belayer tied into the other, and the belayer is often anchored. The belayer pulls the rope through the anchor as the climber ascends, using a belay device to lock off the belay in case of a fall and lowering the climber when the route is completed. The slingshot system has a predictable direction of force and usually provides sufficient friction for the belayer to maintain control easily. Visual and verbal communication are usually easy during the climb, and because the climbers are together at the start it is easy for each to check the knots and belay setup before starting. The slingshot belay is applicable at most outdoor sites and is the most common anchor system in gyms.

The water knot is a retraced overhand knot. Be certain that at least 2-inch tags are left outside the knot and that it's pulled very tight. Check this knot frequently!—the tags have a tendency to creep back into the knot.

Even though straightforward, the slingshot, like any belay, has many details that must be in place for the system to work safely. Leaving out even the smallest details can compromise safety and each climber should become expert at analyzing each setup to be certain that the safest possible system has been established. This involves a fair amount of judgment. You are encouraged to go slowly and if you find yourself doubting the safety of a particular setup then move on to another route.

There are two precautions to take when setting up a slingshot anchor:
1. Do not give in to the temptation to solo an easy route to get to the top and set up your anchor—climbers have been injured or killed doing this. Always take the most secure path to the top, even if that means going the long way around.
2. Consider tying yourself in while you build the anchor. Often this is as easy as girth hitching a long sling to a tree back from the edge and clipping in. I can think of two accidents in the past year when climbers fell off cliffs while building toprope anchors. In one case a man fell 70 feet to the ground and died. In the other, a woman (remarkably) survived a similar fall, though with many broken bones and internal injuries.

> **Tip #7: Setting Up An Anchor**
> • Don't give in to the temptation to solo an easy route to get to the top and set up your anchor—even if it means going the long way around.
> • Consider tying yourself in while you build the anchor.

SECURE anchors culminate in a Master Point (S) that is (E)xtended over the edge, (C)entered over the route, formed by multiple carabiners creating an (U)nbroken ring that is easy for the rope to (R)un through, and has padding on the (E)dge if necessary.

An anchor offers one thing: security. Without a secure anchor it doesn't matter how good the belay setup is or how well that belayer does his or her job. Before utilizing any belay anchor, determine it's security by analyzing each property represented by the letters in the acronym **SECURE** :

S—STRONG
E—EXTENDED
C—CENTERED
U—UNBROKEN
R—RUN
E—EDGE

STRONG—Is the anchor *strong* enough? If it is made up of a single point, is that point strong enough to be the sole anchor? If a tree is used, is it big enough? Six inches in diameter is a good minimum. Is it well-rooted? Trees growing on cliffs are often shallow-rooted in thin pods of soil. A good sign is big roots growing out of cracks in the rock.

If the anchor is a block or boulder, is it stable? Does it have any dangerously sharp edges that should be padded? Is it buried, sitting flat on the surface, or on a plane that slopes toward the edge? Just because it's big doesn't mean it's secure. Several years ago Todd Skinner and Paul Piana were finishing the first free ascent of the Salathé Wall on El Capitan, in California. They were at the very top, belaying off a huge block that had been used as the final anchor for every prior party on the Salathé. Just as they were topping out the block failed and slid off the edge taking Skinner, Piana and their gear with it. Amazingly the ropes weren't cut and they were held by a backup rope.

Bolt anchors should always be made up of two ⅜-inch bolts. Is each bolt hanger flush with the rock and the shaft perpendicular to the face? Does the hanger spin? Is the nut loose? (It's a good idea to keep an adjustable wrench in your pack.) Is the hanger dangerously worn? (This can often be the case on popular routes where people toprope and lower directly off from the anchor bolts.) Are the bolts at least ⅜-inch in diameter? (Old ¼-inch bolts should not be trusted—a strong backup anchor must safeguard two old ¼-inch bolts.)

Regardless of the type of anchor, if you doubt its security at all, either back it up by running a long sling or second rope to another anchor, or choose a different route.

EXTENDED—Is the anchor *extended* over the cliff edge? In order for the belay rope to run freely, the anchor must extend over the edge. Excessive and potentially dangerous friction can result if the anchor is not over edge of the cliff.

CENTERED Is the anchor *centered* over the route? An anchor that is not over the plumb line means that the climber faces a potentially dangerous swing if he or she falls. A swinging fall can also cause the rope to abrade if it rakes the edge—and even a blunt, smooth edge can damage a rope. Once, for a demonstration, I took an intentional fall and the rope scraped no more than 6 inches across a very smooth, rounded edge. The sheath was cut halfway through.

If a centered anchor is not possible, or if the route does not run straight up-and-down, place directional anchors or choose another route.

UNBROKEN Does the *master point* form an *unbroken* ring? The master point is the connection between the anchor and the belay rope and is usually a pair of carabiners. The most common option is to use two oval carabiners that are clipped in so they are reversed and opposed. This means that the gates are aligned so each opens in the opposite direction and one carabiner is spun 180 degrees. The result of this orientation is that an unbroken ring of aluminum is formed, minimizing the possibility that the rope can be pulled across the gates and unclip itself. To test the setup, open both gates: they should cross forming an "X" in the middle. A single carabiner should never be used, even if it's a locker. The following will drive home the point:

"On July 11, 1994 a climber was teaching a person how to rappel. Several successful rappels were completed before the carabiner/sling system failed and the victim fell 20 feet to the ground. Somehow, the carabiner linking the rappel rope to the sling system at the anchor point came unclipped. Though it was a *locking carabiner*, it was not locked—or was inadvertently unlocked." *(Accidents in North American Mountaineering,* 1995. Page 54.)

Other common setups that offer additional security utilize *triple* oval carabiners with each adjoining pair reversed and opposed, or double locking carabiners, reversed, opposed, and locked.

RUN Does the rope *run* smoothly through the master point? Is there too much drag? If so, the anchor may need to be extended farther over the edge. Are there any cracks or projections that can jam the rope? You may need to move the anchor slightly, but remember: keep it as *centered* as possible. One climber should pull the rope from the belay position on the ground to ensure that it is smoothly running, and adjustments should be made as necessary. Moving the belay position on the ground is another option for helping the rope to run freely.

EDGE Does the *edge* need to be padded? Remember, even a smooth, rounded edge can cause severe rope damage. Padding options include placing a pack or some clothing under the anchor at the edge—be sure these items are stable and tied in—or running the rope through a section of old fire hose. (A keeper sling can be run through a hole cut in the hose and clipped in to part of the anchor.)

The Master Point must be formed using multiple carabiners with their gates reversed and opposed. Using just a single carabiner, even a locking one, is dangerous.

A pack makes a great edge pad and is easily held in place utilizing a short piece of cord and a clamping knot on the rope.

Two slings with the lower carabiners reversed is another anchor option especially suited to bolted belays. This setup eliminates the possibility of a shock load if either bolt fails. To minimize force, keep the angle between the slings at the Master Point less than 90°. (See Vectors, Chapter 7.)

A tree girth hitched (top) with the sling forming a straight line through the loop.
A tree incorrectly girth hitched (bottom). A pulley has been formed by the angle of the sling, multiplying the forces unnecessarily.

BASIC ANCHORS

There are several ways to create basic anchors. Trees, boulders, natural chockstones, and solid horns projecting from rock can all be girthhitched with a sling creating a single-loop master point; or, if the anchor point isn't close to the edge, a second rope can be attached and then a figure eight-on-a-bight can be used over the edge as the master point.

If the anchor consists of two bolts there are two options:

1. Clip the bolts together with a sling that has been twisted into a *Magic X*. To do this, clip a carabiner to each bolt and then take a 24-inch sling (use a longer sling if the anchors are more than a foot or so apart), and clip it to each carabiner. There are now two strands of webbing between the two carabiners. Put a half-twist into either of the two strands, forming a small loop. Clip your master point carabiners through this loop and the other strand. In this configuration the twist eliminates the possibility that the master point carabiners will slide off the sling if either of the two bolts fail. Test it to see if you have configured the Magic X correctly. Unclip either of the carabiners attached to the bolt and attempt to slide the master point carabiner off the sling. If it can't come off, the Magic X has been configured correctly. Replace the bolt carabiner. The Magic X is self-equalizing; the master point slides to keep the forces equal on each bolt regardless of the direction of force. A drawback to the Magic X setup is that if either bolt fails, the master point will suddenly extend and shock-load the second bolt.

2. In the second method, two slings are used: one clipped to each bolt with a carabiner. A carabiner is clipped to the bottom of each sling in such a way that when the two are brought together as the master point, they are reversed and opposed. Oval carabiners should be used for the master point, or even better, lockers. This setup eliminates the possibility of a shock load if either bolt fails. To minimize force, keep the angle between the slings at the master point less than 90 degrees. (See Chapter 7.)

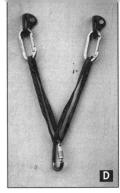

It is common to find a loop of webbing tied through bolt anchors forming the so-called *American Triangle.* It is formed when climbers, usually rappelling off an anchor, untie a sling, run it through the two bolts, and re-tie it creating a triangle of webbing. This configuration creates angles that multiply the forces on the bolts. Do not create or use an American Triangle. If you find an American Triangle and the bolts will still accommodate carabiners, simply rig your anchor ignoring the resident sling. If there are a number of slings through the hangers and you can't clip the bolts, cut the old slings out.

You will often find that the bolt anchor you are using is equipped with chains and a *laplink* (or *rappel ring*—a solid ring about two inches or less in diameter), as the master point. These are found at most sport climbing areas and offer a fully-equipped, pre-equalized anchor. However, belaying and lowering directly off the fixed master point will cause unnecessary wear and these anchors should be rigged with a Magic X.

One option that is available at most toprope sites is to set up two adjacent routes at the same time using one rope. Simply create a SECURE anchor over each route and run the rope up from the ground, through the first anchor, across and through the second anchor, and back down to the ground. Make certain to check any edges the rope will run over. Each climber can try both routes before moving on.

After you have built your anchor, thread your rope through the master point and lower each end to the ground. On short routes there is no need to locate the midpoint of the rope in the anchor—just make sure both ends are on the ground. If lowering the rope ends will not get them to the ground (it may not be possible on slabs or low-angled faces), you will need to toss the ends off. You must be clipped in to an anchor to do this. Starting at the master point, lay arm's-length loops of rope back and forth in one hand until you're holding the entire rope. (This is called a *lap coil*). Separate the coil into two halves and yell, "Rope!" to alert those below you (if it's a crowded site, wait until you hear "Clear!"), toss the half-coil that is closest to the anchor, and when it is down, toss the half-coil containing the ends of the rope. This method works far better than trying to toss the entire coil at once.

The Magic X can be used on any anchor with two pieces.

A. Clip a sling to the carabiner on each piece.

B. Pull the sling between the two carabiners down for form a double "V."

C. Put a full twist in the upper part of the "V" to form a loop.

D. Clip a carabiner(s) through the loop and the lower "V." The Magic X traps the sling so that if either piece fails, the other will hold the load.

BE SCARED

An American Triangle. Avoid these if you value your life.

How Do Bolts and Pitons Work?

Like all anchors, bolts and pitons rely primarily on friction and wedging for their holding power. When you use them, you are trusting that the person who put them in understood how to maximize their holding power and placed them correctly.

bolts—Rely primarily on the friction between the shaft of the bolt and the rock. Their strength can be augmented by the use of expanding cones to help them wedge in the hole or epoxy that bonds the shaft to the rock; and bolts are strongest when loaded perpendicular to their shaft. Bolts come in many designs and several manufacturers make bolts specifically for use as toprope belay anchors. Since bolts are "fixed" (i.e. permanent) and difficult to visually assess for reliability, always back them up when you can.

pitons—Rely on a combination of friction and wedging. Like a nail in a board, friction between the piton and the rock provides substantial strength. This is increased when the orientation is perpendicular to the anticipated force. Pitons that are made of U-shaped pieces of metal also provide a wedging action as the metal "springs" against the rock as it is driven. Pitons, like bolts, are typically fixed in place; back them up whenever possible.

How Can You Tell If Bolts and Pitons Can Be Trusted?

Never trust fixed anchors without inspecting them. Fixed anchors fail and climbers die. Treat fixed anchors like food you find in the back of the refrigerator: always be suspicious; when you take a close look be prepared to back up, and if it stinks, don't touch it. With any fixed anchor, always back it up with a good chock, cam, or natural anchor if you can.

bolts—Familiarize yourself with modern bolt and hanger styles, and be suspicious of any you find that appear old or have homemade hangers. Check the guidebook for the first ascent date, a good gauge of the bolt's age. Check the diameter, if it is less than 3/8-inch, be wary. Check the quality of the hole and the placement; the hole should be clean-cut without coning, and perpendicular to the surface. The hanger should be flush and tight. Look for signs of damage or wear. Some hangers wear incredibly fast if they are lowered off of frequently.

pitons—Look for excessive rust or a bent or cracked eye. Check to see if it is tightly placed. This requires a hammer and a light tap. It should ring: if it sounds hollow, look out. Look for fractures around the placement—over-driven pitons can crack the rock to the point where the placement is compromised. Compare the piton's orientation with the anticipated direction of force. Pitons are strongest when loaded perpendicular to the shaft and the crack. Beware of pitons that will be loaded parallel with the crack: they are inherently weaker.

If the eye is not flush, consider tying the piton off with a short sling. (See the Knot section in this chapter.)

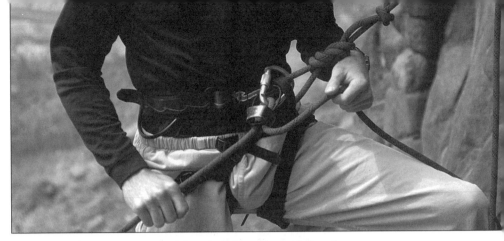

A belayer ready to CATCH is tied tightly to the belay anchor and aligned with the anticipated direction of force. This belayer communicates with the climber and has the brake hand on the rope.

BASIC BELAYING PRINCIPLES

With a *secure* anchor built and both ends of the rope on the ground you are ready to establish the belay. Climbers sometimes reach this point safely but then fail to follow the basic principles of belaying and thus put themselves and others in danger. In order to maximize safety, the principles outlined here must be followed every time you belay.

Before allowing the climber to start, be certain that you are ready to **CATCH** a fall:

C— CLOSED SYSTEM
A— ANCHORED & ALIGNED
T— TIGHT
C— COMMUNICATION
H— HAND ON THE ROPE

CLOSED SYSTEM—Is the belayer part of a closed system? This is easily accomplished by tying in to the other end of the rope. This is an excellent, and in some cases life-saving, habit to get into as it ensures that the belayer will never drop the climber by letting the end of the rope slip through the belay. The following story should reinforce this point:
"Two climbers had...climbed the bolted route *Knucklehead* and (one) was being lowered by (another) who was belaying at the base. When (the climber) was most of the way down the end of the rope suddenly slipped through the belay plate and (the climber) fell about three meters to the ground." *Accidents in North American Mountaineering*, 1995, page 46. In this accident the climber was very fortunate, in other cases climbers have died.

ANCHORED & ALIGNED—Is the belayer *anchored?* It is strongly recommended that the belayer on the ground be anchored to ensure that he or she cannot be pulled off balance and lose control of the belay. This is often as easy as

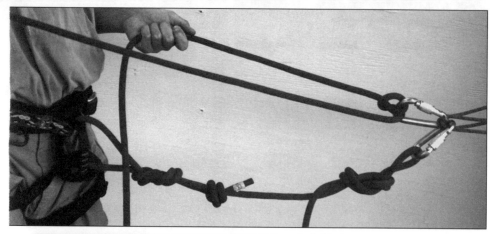

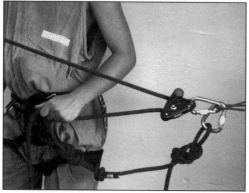

A Munter Hitch (top) or GriGri (bottom) are good choices when the belayer needs to be away from the anchor (See Chapter 6).

girth hitching a tree and clipping the belayer in with a locking carabiner.

I once saw what can happen when the belayer on the ground is not anchored. The belayer was sitting on a log about ten feet from the cliff, reclining comfortably against another tree with her feet dangling a couple of feet off the ground. When her partner fell she was launched from her seat, flew through the air, and impacted the cliff with her face. To her credit she never dropped the climber, but the incident did put an early end to their day.

Though highly recommended, it is not always necessary to be anchored when belaying on the ground. When the belayer is much heavier than the climber or when friction in the system is high enough that complete control is easy, it may be okay to belay unanchored—use your best judgment; when in doubt, tie the belayer in.

Is the belayer *aligned* with the anticipated direction of force? It's good to remember your ABCs: a straight line should be formed between the anchor, the belayer, and the force on the climber. An appropriately positioned belayer is lined up with the anchor and braced to catch a fall.

TIGHT—Is the belayer *tight* to the anchor? Aligned with the anchor is not enough. In order to maintain control the belayer should be tight to the anchor and in line with the anticipated direction of force. Even with as little as a couple of feet of slack it is possible for the belayer to be pulled off balance.

To test if the belayer is *aligned* and *tight*, have the climber weight the rope before leaving the ground. Under tension, the belayer will find exactly the right position. It helps if the footing is solid and easy for the belayer. If the ground is uneven, adjust the ground anchor position or the belayer's tie-in length to find the most stable stance.

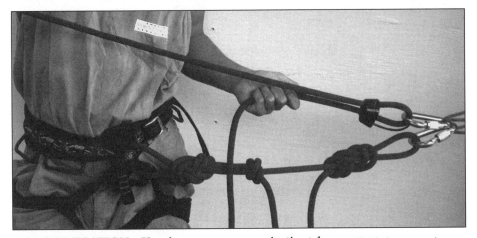

COMMUNICATION—Has the proper *communication* taken place between the climber and belayer? It is essential that both the climber and belayer are clear on what is going to happen. Do both understand the signals? Do they know what the plan is when the climber reaches the top? Will the climber walk off, or lower off? Have all distractions been eliminated and is the belayer ready to focus on belaying? Will the belayer pay particular attention during the first 15 feet of the route to prevent rope stretch injuries if the climber falls? (See Chapter 6.) Have both checked each other's knot; the anchor; and the belay?

HAND ON THE ROPE—It is vital that the brake hand never leave the rope. If the belayer lets go with the break hand, the climber has no belay. Can the belayer feed out rope and take in rope while keeping the break hand on the rope at all times? Is the belayer prepared to catch a fall? Can he/she hold the climber's weight as long as necessary? Can the belayer lower the climber safely? An affirmative to each of these questions is only possible if the proper hand movements take place.

Four definitions are necessary before discussing the mechanics. The end of the rope the climber is tied into is called the live end; the end the belayer is tied to is called the standing end; the hand doing the actual belaying is called the brake hand; the free hand is called the guide hand. When belaying with a plate, tube or Figure 8 device, the mechanics are the same:

1. Move the rope through the belay device by pulling the live end of the rope toward the device with the guide hand while pulling the standing end of the rope away from the device using the brake hand.
2. Slide the guide hand along the live end—away from the device.
3. Using the brake hand, place the standing end into the guide hand.
4. Slide the brake hand along the standing end toward the device.
5. Drop the standing end from the guide hand.
6. Repeat.

BASIC BELAY METHODS

Assuming a SECURE anchor has been built and that the principles necessary to CATCH a fall are understood and will be put into use, the last decision concerns where to attach the belay device. Two attachment points are available: the belayer's harness or the ground anchor itself.

When the two attachment points are compared, belaying off the harness has several advantages:
• For most people it is the most natural position.
• The belay device will be in the correct position to operate.
• Extra tension can be given to the climber by squatting.
• It prepares the belayer for belaying future leads.
• Fall factors are lower—the belayer absorbs some force.

Belaying off a ground anchor also has several advantages:
• It is easier for the belayer to hold the climber's weight for long periods (working routes).
• Escaping the belay is much easier (see Chapter 7).
• Being *aligned* and *tight* to the anchor is guaranteed.

Belaying off the anchor, however, has disadvantages:
• It requires a solid ground anchor (trees are best).
• The belayer must stay in position to lock the device in case of a fall—even moving a couple of feet ahead of the anchor can make the device ineffective.
• Fall factors are higher because the anchor will not "give."

If the choice is made to belay off the anchor, the device should be situated at waist height and the belayer should be positioned so they can effectively operate the device. If the belayer must stand a few feet away from the anchor, extend the master point by tying a figure 8-on-a-bight on the standing end of the rope the same distance from the anchor as the belayer is.

Belaying from an extended master point.

PRE-CLIMB CHECK

At this point we have established a SECURE slingshot anchor at the top of the route, anchored and positioned the belayer to CATCH a fall, and chosen the most appropriate belay method—the climber is almost ready to leave the ground. Before he or she does so, take the following precautions:

1. Do a buddy check of all buckles, knots and the belay. The top slingshot anchor should be checked by both climbers at the time it is set up.
2. Make sure that both climbers agree on the plan for the ascent (i.e., climb to anchor, lower off).
3. Make sure both climbers understand and agree on the signals to be used. (At crowded areas it is wise to use names.)

Description of Basic Signals

- **On Belay**...tells the climber that the belay is in effect, a fall will be caught from that point on, and he or she may begin climbing.
- **Climbing**...tells the belayer that the climber has started.
- **Climb Away**...tells the climber that the belayer knows he or she is climbing. Don't climb until you hear this. It is confirmation that the belayer is paying attention. Climbers have been hurt falling in the first few feet of a climb because the belayer was not aware they had started.
- **Slack**...is asked for when rope is too tight. Be careful. Novices will often yell, "Take up the slack," but the belayer may only hear "Slack!," and give the climber the opposite of what is desired. Then the climber will probably yell, "Take up the slack!" even louder! Be sure to get this signal straight before starting.
- **Up Rope**...means that too much slack has developed and the climber wants the belayer to take it in.
- **Tension**...means that the climber wants a very tight rope to feel secure.
- **Watch Me**...signals the belayer that the climber is at a tough move and might fall.
- **Falling!**...means that the climber is actually falling or, just as likely, that he or she is about to fall. (*Ahhh!* This is what climbers actually say when they are falling—at least, I use it frequently).
- **Take**...means almost the same thing as "Falling!" It is a sport climbing term that means: "I'm letting go, please lock off the belay." Then the climber typically takes a very short lead fall (less than five feet).
- **On Rappel**...tells others that the climber is about to rappel (and alerts those giving a fireman's belay—see the Rappelling section.)
- **Off Belay**...tells the belayer that the climber is anchored or on the ground.
- **Off Rappel**...means that the rappeller is no longer attached to the rope and is anchored or on the ground.

- **Rope**...when yelled from above, tells others that rope is about to be dropped. The climber should wait to hear "Clear!" before tossing the rope if climbing at a crowded area.
- **Clear**...is the answer to "Rope!" and means the area is clear and it's okay to drop the rope
- **Rock**...means "Look out! Something may drop on your head!" (See Sight Considerations chapter.)

BASIC CLIMBING OPTIONS

There are many things you can do while toproping to help develop skills and increase the fun level. Trying progressively harder routes is the most common option, but it can get dull. Here are just 20 possibilities, many of them involving friendly competition. Feel free to innovate:
- Toproping can be used to work a route prior to a lead.
- See who can do a route using the fewest holds.
- Do the same route using the most holds.
- Eliminate certain holds to increase the grade. You'll be amazed when "key" holds are no longer needed—it means you're getting better!
- On a crack climb, make every possible jam.
- Even more challenging, climb a crack using just the surrounding face holds.
- Climb a route blindfolded, with the belayer giving directions—it makes you aware of body position and balance like never before.
- Play "Simon Says" with the belayer giving you the hold sequences—don't worry, you can get even later.
- Get every possible no-hands rest.
- Do a dynamic move statically—this will help increase your strength and control.
- Downclimb a route—this ability will be very helpful when working through sequences in the future.
- Do laps up and down with no rest—this builds endurance.
- Find lunge moves—the belayer will have to be really on his or her toes for this.
- Make every step a high step—this will improve your balance and flexibility.
- Don't use any handholds above your shoulders—it helps you learn to trust your feet.
- Climb an easy route with just one hand or one foot—great for balance training.
- Do as many cross-over and step-through moves as possible.
- Traverse back and forth all the way up the route—watch out for swing potential.
- Use all sidepulls or undercling holds.
- Use crack systems at the base of climbs to practice gear placement and anchor building.

Basic Safety Management

The key to maintaining the safest possible climbing environment is to take all necessary precautions while approaching the site, while climbing,and on the descent—all the while staying prepared for emergencies.

BASIC PREPARATIONS

- Have paper and pencil with you. This will allow you to write instructions down to be given to emergency personnel by a runner. I remember watching an ambulance lose precious minutes driving to the wrong trailhead because a flustered runner had muffled verbal instructions.
- Tell someone your plans. But don't leave a note on your car that says, "Off to do 'Idiot Crack,' back at 4 P.M." The local thief will translate this as, "Idiots climbing crack, take all you want."
- Have emergency phone numbers with you—local police, hospital, technical rescue team, climbing shop. Minutes count in an accident and you don't want to be running around looking for a phone book. Keep the phone list and your car keys in the same pocket of your pack and tell your partner where they are.
- Bring a first aid kit. Excellent first aid kits designed for climbers are available from several manufacturers. Also, bring extra water, a jacket, a knife, a cigarette lighter, a chocolate bar or two, and in appropriate circumstances, a compass, and a headlamp with fresh batteries!

I once learned a painful lesson about keeping my emergency equipment functional. A bunch of us were in the parking lot below Cannon Cliff in New Hampshire, preparing to head up the huge talus slope to recover a severely injured climber. Time was critical and we were all moving really fast to get ready. To my dismay I found that while my headlamp had fresh batteries in it, the strap was broken. No sooner had I made my dilemma known to some of the other rescuers than I found my headlamp securely fastened to my head— with a couple of passes of duct tape. Off we went, hurrying into the night. It was summer and we all got sweaty and the tape pulled my hair a little, but in the excitement of it all I hardly noticed.

We reached the base of the cliff to find two climbers on the ground. The leader had taken a 40-footer and lost the rack near the top of the cliff. The belayer had self-rescued, managing to descend five pitches with his semi-conscious partner, much of it in the dark, with almost no gear. We packaged the injured climber and ferried him down the talus. We later learned that his injuries included a skull fracture, punctured lung and liver, many broken ribs, a broken arm and internal bleeding. They told us that another hour would have killed him. When it was over and we were all sitting in the parking lot waiting for the adrenaline to wear off, someone (I have my suspicions) walked up behind me and said, "Rescue's over Peter," and ripped the headlamp from my head.

No one likes a rescue. To reduce risk:

- Use a backup belayer when appropriate and available. A backup belayer simply feeds the rope to the primary belayer. If the climber falls and the primary belayer loses control, the backup belayer can catch the fall. This is a very easy system backup and is particularly appropriate with a novice belayer, youth, or a very light belayer.
- Have everyone, whether climbing, belaying, or just on the ground, wear a helmet. One day I was working on the upper section of an overhanging finger crack at Golden Cliffs, in Colorado. The bucket of my dreams appeared in the form of a brick-sized flake poking out of the crack. The top of it was incut and I latched onto it without hesitation. I yarded. It creaked and came out in my hand. I was directly above my partner, Charley, but had just enough control of the flake before I let it go to steer it away from him. I watched it arc into the talus a few feet from where Charley sat. If I had not had that moment of influence on that flake, if it had just popped out and gone straight down, it could easily have hit Charley in the head. Wearing a helmet he might have withstood a blow like that and held the fall, giving both of us just a scary story. But without a helmet the flake could have severely injured or killed him and a few moments later I would have crashed into the talus from 70 feet. Wear your helmet—even when belaying.
- Keep your rope neat and always operate off the top of the pile. A poorly stacked rope will not feed out properly and a tangled rope can create a dangerous situation.
- Tie in while setting up the top anchor. This has been said before but it is worth repeating. Climbers fall off cliffs while setting up toprope climbs.

I heard a horrifying story one day from a fellow guide. He watched a pair of climbers preparing to do a popular 5.10 route called Reverse Camber at the top of Cathedral Ledge in New Hampshire. The route climbs a beautiful 50-foot face with 350 feet of breathtaking exposure and is often toproped. The anchor is a big maple tree 50 feet back from the edge and most folks fix a rope on the tree, clip in, and walk down to the edge to belay. On this day however, for some unknown reason, one climber walked down to the very edge of the cliff, uncoiled part of the rope, tied an end in to her harness, and then chucked the coil off into space. (My fingers are sweating as I type this!) The guide said he had a perfect view of the rope tangling in mid-air, forming a big blob. He said that as the blob fell he was certain that the climber would be yanked off the top for a 4-second free-fall into the talus. Miraculously, that didn't happen. The rope hung up on the slab and the climber pulled it back up to untangle it. She seemed unaware of how close a call it was.

When climbing with a novice partner, or when introducing a friend to the sport, take as much time as necessary to familiarize him or her with the systems before you leave the ground. Have him or her practice belaying and make certain the mechanics are understood and can be performed without letting go of the brake hand. Have that person hold your weight and then catch you just off the ground. Provide the easiest device to belay with. Always double-check knots and buckles. Let him or her also put body weight on the rope just off the ground to develop trust in the system. Make sure it's known that there is no such thing as a stupid question, and that you are listening. Use a backup belayer if possible. Go over the signals. Don't leave the ground until you are certain that your student or friend understands and can perform the basic functions.

Always close the system by having the belayer tie in to the end of the rope.

Troubleshooting

By necessity, troubleshooting will be limited here. For information on self-rescue techniques please consult David Fasulo's *Self-Rescue* (Falcon Press: Helena, MT, 1998). If you are not absolutely sure you can deal with a situation safely, don't try. Get help instead.

- The rope gets stuck while climbing—even when diligent in setting up the top anchor the rope occasionally gets stuck. The first thing to do is have the climber stop before any slack develops. Try to determine what is hanging the rope up—often a tug from the belayer in the right direction of the climber weighting the rope will pop it free. If this doesn't work, ask others nearby for help.
- The rope gets stuck while retrieving it from the anchor. This can happen for a variety of reasons but is usually simple to fix. Analyze and try tugging. If a climber can be safely tied in at the anchor, try going up there and working the rope from above. Do not try to ascend a stuck rope. If you are competent at rappelling and a second rope is available, rappel the route and free the rope. Always use a backup when rappelling. If this doesn't work, ask others nearby for help.
- The rope tangles while climbing or lowering. Again, this can also be avoided by stacking the rope and always working from the top of the pile. Have the climber stop climbing, or, if lowering, ask him or her to try to find a stance and un-weight the rope. Untangle the rope without endangering the climber.

Being prepared, taking precautions and being able to troubleshoot simple problems is the first step to climbing responsibly. However, without additional skills, you will be limited to climbing areas where the basic slingshot belay is easy to set up—if there are any complicating factors, you may not be able to get yourself out of a jam. Suppose you want to toprope the last pitch of a 500-foot climb that is right at your ability limit.

How do you help ensure that the climber will be protected while being lowered to the start of the climb? If the belayer knows how to use a clamping knot back-up then you can lower over the abyss confidently.

What happens if 50 feet from the top you hit a move you just can't do? If your belayer knows how to do a dropped loop assisted raise they can have you past that move in just a couple of minutes. If they don't, but you have some cord with you and know how to rig an improvised ascender then you can get past the move yourself.

Suppose your partner lowers you down to the end of the rope and you can't make the first move? Embarrassing to say the least; potentially dangerous if you can't ascend the rope and your partner doesn't know how to rig a 3:1 haul system.

Suppose you're in the same situation, you get hurt and there is no one else around to help. If the belayer cannot escape the belay and go for help then no one will come until someone notices you are missing.

Several years ago two climbers trapped themselves at the top of the *Wiessner Route* on Cannon Cliff in New Hampshire. The belayer was at the top of the cliff but the second could not make the last strenuous move fifty feet below him. Though they had all the gear they needed, neither of them had any self-rescue expertise. The second could not rig an improvised ascender and climb five feet up the rope to easy ground, the belayer did not know how to do a dropped loop assisted raise, could not rig a 3:1 haul system and did not know how to escape the belay. All they could do was yell for help. Hours later help arrived and in just a few moments the second climber was safely at the top. If no one had heard their cries or if it had rained that night, they might have died from hypothermia. They were in over their heads. Don't make the same mistakes.

Self-rescue is beyond the scope of this book. Before you go beyond the basic slingshot toprope system, take the time to read David Fasulo's book. Then practice the techniques on the ground. If possible, get professional instruction. Learning fundamental self-rescue skills will save your life.

Advanced Equipment

Caution: Don't use equipment you're unfamiliar with! Using advanced gear requires advanced judgment. Get proper training if you're unsure of your proficiency with a particular piece of equipment.

CORD

Like webbing, cord is used to make and extend connections. But webbing and cord are not always interchangeable.

Cord is made up of various materials including Perlon™, Spectra™ and Vectran™. Cord is purchased by the foot and tied by the user using a double or triple fisherman's knot. Cord cannot be sewn.

Like the climbing rope, cord uses kernmantle construction. The same care and damage assessment principles apply. Cord comes in sizes ranging from 3mm to 9mm with 5.5 to 7mm being the most useful. Because Perlon is not as strong as others, use only 6mm or larger. Spectra, Vectran and some other materials are stronger and can be used in their smaller 5.5mm size. For most toprope applications, two 24-inch cord slings and one *cordelette* are all that will be needed in addition to the regular assortment of slings.

The common uses for cord include:
- Prussik slings—5.5 or 6mm, 14 to 24 inches long.
- 6- to 8-foot tied loops called cordelettes are used to build anchors and in rescue situations.
- Slings—8mm or larger diameters, though cord has lower abrasion resistance than sewn runners. Take caution when using over an edge.

ADVANCED BELAY AND RAPPEL DEVICES

GriGri

This is the original self-locking belay device. It works on the same principle as the seat belts in your car: the inertia from a sudden load activates a cam that pinches the rope off and holds it fast. Tension is released and controlled by a spring-loaded lever. The GriGri has several advantages:
- Self-activating when suddenly loaded (but the basic principle that the brake hand never leaves the rope still applies).
- Requires no hand strength to hold the climber for extended periods of time.

The GriGri uses a camming mechanism to stop the rope automatically in the case of a fall.

- Works great when belaying directly off the anchor. Keep the side with the tension-release lever facing out. This keeps the lever from being accidentally activated while belaying.
- Easily incorporated into a self-rescue system.

And several disadvantages:
- The GriGri is heavy compared to plates and tubes.
- Costs a lot more.
- If threaded backwards, there is no belay whatsoever.
- Lowering is awkward until you get the hang of it.
- Řappelling is awkward and convenient only on a single rope.
- Easier to "juice" a leader (shortrope them).
- If the climber begins moving too fast while being lowered, the proper technique is to let go of the tension-release lever. This is opposite of the natural tendency, especially of novice belayers, to pull harder on the lever—and climbers have been dropped because of this.

Munter Hitch

This is not a device at all, but rather a hitch wherein the rope itself acts as the braking device. (See Chapter 7.) The munter hitch works by looping the rope around itself and a carabiner in such a way that it feeds easily while unloaded, but flips and locks securely under tension. The munter hitch is a very simple and effective belay method and has the following advantages:
- It is secure and appropriate on any terrain or on routes of any difficulty.
- It only requires an HMS (pear-shaped) locking carabiner.
- It can be used for both belaying and rappelling.
- The belayer does not have to be right next to it to activate it—it can be operated remotely.

The only disadvantages are:
- It can twist the rope.
- If made backwards (with the loaded strand on the gate side instead of on the spine side) it is possible that the hitch could rub against the locking mechanism on a screwgate and inadvertently unlock it.

How to build a Munter Hitch.

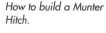

How Protection Works

In the perfect toprope world every route would have either an oak tree or two big bolts at the top of it. Making SECURE anchors would be a snap and we would all save enough money on equipment to spend our winters in Thailand. But not all great routes come with anchors. The ability to construct anchors yourself will greatly expand your route selection possibilities.

Constructed Anchors:
The Principle Behind The Holding Power

All constructed anchors rely on two basic principles for their holding power: friction and wedging. In order to build the strongest anchors possible it is important to understand how each type of anchor utilizes these principles.

Passive Anchors:
No Moving Parts

NUTS. Nuts, a generic term for all hand placed anchors, rely primarily on wedging. There are many designs, all engineered to work by wedging in an irregularity in a crack or pocket—like a cork in a bottle. Typical examples include Wild Country Rocks® and Black Diamond Stoppers®. Some, like Lowe Tricams® and Black Diamond Hexentrics®, incorporate a camming action as well.

Wild Country Rock

A perfect nut placement.

Wild Country Friend

A perfect cam placement.

Active Anchors: Moving Parts

SPRING LOADED CAMMING DEVICES. Spring Loaded Camming Devices (SLCD's or "cams") rely primarily on mechanical wedging for their holding power. Various designs use spring-loaded cams.

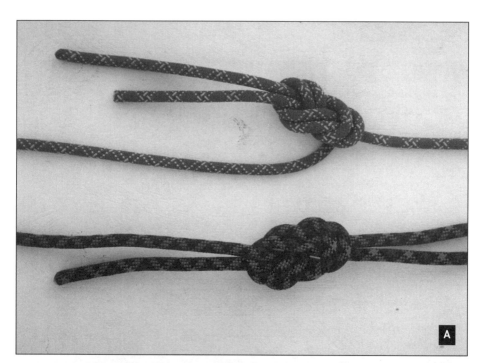

A. Two ways to join two ropes: 1) figure 8 tied in parallel on a bight and 2) figure 8 retraced in opposition. (Leave at least 6-inch tails.)

B. Two more ways to join two ropes: 1) the double fisherman and 2) overhand-on-a-bight used to join two ropes. When using the overhand-on-a-bight, it is especially important that the knot be neat, tight and with tails at least 12-inches long.

Advanced Toprope Systems

While the basic slingshot toprope system works well in many areas. In order to climb competently in areas where the basic system can't be used, advanced skills will be needed.

ADVANCED KNOTS AND HITCHES

Figure Eight

- Can be tied two ways to join rope ends together (for rappelling or toproping routes longer than half-a-pitch).
- Retraced in opposition—leave a minimum of 6-inch tails.
- Tied in parallel on a bight—leave a minimum of 12-inch tails for low-force situations like rappelling.

Double Bowline

- Sometimes used as a tie-in knot.
- Unsafe unless backed up with a double fisherman knot.
- Is useful for tying in to the middle of a rope when toproping routes greater than half-a-pitch.

Double Fisherman

- Commonly used as a joining knot.
- Has great holding power.
- Hard to undo if heavily loaded.
- Use tripled on cord less than 8mm in diameter.

Overhand-on-a-Bight

- Used as a clip-in knot it works fine, but it's harder to undo than a figure eight-on-a-bight.
- As a joining knot in low-force situations like rappelling. A simple, secure knot—leave a minimum of 12-inch tails. The knot must be neat, with no twists and pulled very tight before using.

Clove Hitch

- Used as a clip-in knot, it is fast, easy, and adjustable, but not adequate for high-force situations.
- For tying protection points in opposition. Fast, secure and eliminates multiplication of forces.
- For tying off pitons, trees, etc.—reduces leverage.

The Clove Hitch

A. Make two loops
   ("ears") in the rope

B. Put the rightmost loop
   behind the other

C. Clip biner through
   loops

Girth Hitch

- For tying off pitons, trees, etc.—reduces leverage.
- To attach a sling to a harness for an anchor tether.

Prussik/Autoblock/Kleimheist

- These hitches are used as clamps on the rope and with a few exceptions can be used interchangeably. They are most often used to ascend a fixed rope, to back up rappels, and as components of self-rescue systems. Cord or 9/16-inch webbing will work. (Do not use Spectra™ webbing because it's too slick to give adequate grip.) Throughout the rest of the book the term *clamping hitch* will be used when any of the three are called for. The differences between them are:
  Prussik Very secure, great holding power, can be hard to loosen, must be tied neatly.
  Autoblock Easy to attach, lower holding power than the prussik; very easy to unload; does not need to be attached neatly, easy hitch to use for rappel backup.
  Kleimheist Similar to the autoblock, has greater holding power than the autoblock but less than the prussik; does not need to be attached neatly; easy rappel backup.

The Prussik is formed by passing a cord loop through itself 3 or 4 times around the rope. It is very secure but can be hard to loosen.

An Autoblock is formed by passing a cord loop around the rope 3 to 5 times and clipping the ends together. It has the least holding power of the clamping knots and is best suited to backing up a rappel.

Munter Hitch

- Excellent for belaying and if you drop your device! Requires HMS carabiner; can be used for rappelling but twists the rope. (See photos, page 48.)

Mule Knot

- Used as a releasable blocking knot in self-rescue systems. (See photos, page 54.)

The Klemheist is formed like the Autoblock but the bottom loop is passed through the top loop before clipping with a carabiner.

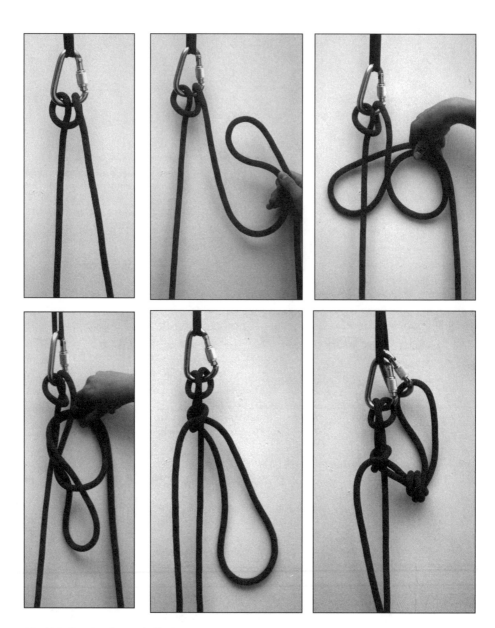

The Mule Knot is a fast and effective
way of creating a releasable blocking
knot. Here it is shown backing up a
Munter Hitch belay off the anchor. The
Mule Knot should be backed up with
an overhand knot clipped into the anchor
to ensure security.

ADVANCED ANCHORS AND BELAYS

In the Basic Anchors and Belays section we covered single-point anchors (trees, blocks) and double-bolt anchors. This section will cover multi-point anchors, both natural as well as those constructed using nuts and cams. A working knowledge of protection placement techniques is assumed.

It is beneficial here to start by re-emphasizing the need for every belay anchor to be **SECURE.** (The acronym SECURE replaces that of SRENE. Die-hard SRENEies can still use it.) For an anchor to be **SECURE,** it must be: *strong; extended* over the edge; *centered* over the climb with the master point forming an *unbroken* ring of aluminum; the rope freely *running;* and the *edge* padded if necessary. The most cleverly constructed belay anchor is worth nothing if it is not SECURE.

A cordelette used to form an ERNEST anchor consisting of Black Diamond Camelot, a Metolius FCU and a Wild Country Rock.

When it comes to constructing multipoint anchors, yet another acronym will be helpful—**ERNEST**. A product of the brilliant mind of guide Marc Chauvin, **ERNEST** stands for:

E— **EQUALIZED**
R— **REDUNDANT**
NE—**NO EXTENSION**
S— **SOLID AND STABLE**
T— **TIMELY**

All climbers should construct belay anchors in **ERNEST**:

EQUALIZED Are the anchor points *equalized*? Do they all share the load as equally as possible? Though each individual anchor point should be strong, sharing the load diversifies the risk—like investing in mutual funds. Methods for equalizing anchor points will be described below.

REDUNDANT Is the anchor *redundant*? Is it made up of a minimum of two and preferably more individual anchor points? A well constructed anchor should always consist of more than one piece.

NO EXTENSION If one anchor point fails will there be *no extension* in the system to shock-load the other pieces? Techniques for minimizing or eliminating extension will be described below.

SOLID AND STABLE Is each anchor point *solid*? Is every component correctly seated and *stable*? Are nuts and cams placed such that they will be loaded in their strongest orientation? Is each component in line with the anticipated direction of force? Do all the anchor points act as a unit when the system is loaded? You may have to adjust the equalization.

Placement Assessment

With the exception of bolts, all anchor placements rely on some kind of crack—and cracks signify weakness. When placing cams or nuts to build an anchor keep the following points in mind:

- *Be sure the walls of the crack are solid and that neither is just part of a tottering block.*
- *Be sure the rock is not crumbly—rotten rock generally means a rotten anchor.*

After you have judged the crack to be stable and the rock solid you must determine what types of hand-placed anchors to use. Does the crack have constrictions and irregularities? If so, Rocks®, Stoppers®, Tri-cams® or Hexentrics® may work best.

- *Use the largest anchors possible—larger anchors distribute the load over a wider area and use stronger wires or webbing.*
- *Place anchors with as much surface area contact as possible— this gives greater holding power and stability.*
- *Try to fit the anchor precisely to the constriction or irregularity— make every placement look like the illustration in the equipment catalogs.*
- *Be sure the anchor is stable and that it will be loaded in its strongest orientation.*

Does the crack have smooth, parallel walls? If so, the camming units may work best. They are easy and fast to place and their range of motion makes it less necessary to get a precise fit. However, they are only reliable if placed correctly:

- *Use the correct size for the crack—the best fit is achieved when the cams are retracted about halfway through their range of motion—too tight and the cam may become "fixed," which means that you have to go buy another one; too loose and it may "walk" out of position and become unreliable.*
- *Orient the shaft parallel with the anticipated direction of force— if it is pulled into alignment later it may lose its security.*
- *Avoid placements where one set of cams is tightly retracted and the other is open—this is inherently weaker and less stable.*
- *Be sure the cams are all properly positioned—cams that become "inverted" (twisted completely out of position) greatly reduces security.*
- *Avoid placements where the stem will be stressed over an edge.*
- *Avoid the tendancy to rely too much on cams—they should not be the default; analyze each placement and use the most appropriate type of anchor.*

TIMELY Is the anchor *timely*? Has the anchor been built where it should be? Is it within view? Above the climber? Does the rope run with minimal drag? Will communication be easy? An untimely toprope belay anchor would be one that is too far away for easy communication (both sight and verbal), requires multiple directionals, or produces unacceptable drag. The key to making a toprope belay anchor *timely* is to make it *secure*.

Let's use three scenarios to illustrate some of the methods you can use to be *ernest*.

SCENARIO #1

STEP 1 You have located two trees five feet apart and ten feet back from the edge directly over your route. Their number and position make the belay *redundant* and *timely*. You have determined that each tree is big enough to be *solid* and rooted well enough to be *stable*. So that leaves you with *equalized* and *no extension* to take care of. You have two basic options for accomplishing these last tasks: using long slings or a second rope. In either case the first step is to either wrap or girth hitch a sling around the base of each tree and clip a locking carabiner to each one. (Remember to be tied in while you are working near the edge.) If you choose long slings, here are the steps :

STEP 2 Clip a sling—if you have some long enough, or girth hitched slings—into each anchor so the end reaches over the edge.

STEP 3 Form the master point by clipping both loops with reversed and opposed carabiners (double, double-lockers, or triple). If either sling were to fail, there would be no shock-load on the second slings because there is *no extension*.

STEP 4 Verify that when the master point is loaded, the anchor is equalized; that it still meets the *secure* criteria of *centered* over the route; *extended* far enough for the rope to *run* easily, and that the *edge* is padded as necessary. Adjust as needed until it's right.

You can also use a second rope to equalize anchors like these. This technique is especially useful when the anchor points are far from the edge.

STEP 1 Tie a figure eight-on-a-bight on one end of the second rope and clip it to one of the anchor trees. Tie another figure eight loop so that it hangs over the edge properly. This forms half of the master point.

STEP 2 On the slack end, tie another figure eight loop right next to the first. This will form the other half of the master point. Tying two figure eight loops doubles the abrasion resistance, and provides two, independent, full-strength anchor points.

STEP 3 Run the slack end back to the second anchor, tie the last figure eight loop and clip it in.

STEP 4 Clip your master point carabiners through the two figure eight loops over the edge.

STEP 5 Verify security as in Step 3 above.

What About Fixed Anchors?

Never trust fixed anchors without inspecting them. Fixed anchors fail and climbers die. Treat fixed anchors like food you find in the back of the refrigerator, always be suspicious. When you take a close look be prepared to back up, and if it stinks, don't touch it. With any fixed anchor, always back it up with a good chock, cam, or natural anchor if you can.

Bolts Familiarize yourself with modern bolt and hanger styles, and be suspicious of old or homemade hangers.

- Check the guidebook for the first ascent date, a good gauge of the bolt's age.
- Check the diameter, if it is less than ⅜-inch, be wary.
- Check the quality of the hole and the placement; the hole should be clean-cut without coning, and perpendicular to the surface. The hanger should be flush and tight.
- Look for signs of wear. Some hangers wear incredibly fast if they are lowered off of frequently.

Pitons Look for excessive rust or a bent or cracked eye.

- Check to see if it is tightly placed. This requires a hammer and a light tap. It should ring: if it sounds hollow, look out.
- Look for fractures around the placement—over-driven pitons can crack the rock to the point where the placement is compromised.
- Compare the piton's orientation with the anticipated direction of force. Pitons are strongest when loaded perpendicular to the shaft and the crack. Beware of pitons that will load parallel with the crack: they are inherently weaker.

Fixed Chocks Or Cams (AKA Booty)

Friends® were the first cams, invented by the legendary Yosemite climber Ray Jardine over two decades ago. Since then the principle has been refined and is represented by many designs: Wild Country Friends® (they look remarkably like Jardine's first cams; testimony to visionary design), Metolius Three Cam Units® or Black Diamond Camelots®. Hidden in the design of all cams is an invisible wedge created by the angle of the cam against the rock. This angle is kept constant throughout the range of the cam, giving it consistent holding power and a wide range of placement options. Cams do not rely on irregularities in a crack and thus are often the best choice in smooth, parallel-sided cracks.

Assess the quality of the placement and the condition of the piece. Fixed chocks and cams often suffer from the abuse they received when the owners (and subsequent climbers) tried to get them out. If the wires are frayed or the piece is excessively deformed, don't rely on it! I've seen cams battered so badly that it's almost impossible to tell what brand they are.

SCENARIO #2

In the second scenario you are going to construct an anchor consisting of three perfect protection placements, A, B, & C, using a multiple Magic X. Remember that you can minimize potential extension by tying overhand knots in each sling above the equalization point.

STEP 1 Using non-locking carabiners, equalize points A and B using the Magic X. (See the Basic Anchors section for details on how to do this.)

STEP 2 Equalize points B and C. You have now reduced the three points to two.

STEP 3 Equalize these last two points and clip in your master point carabiners.

SCENARIO #3

The setup described above is effective but uses three slings and at least five carabiners in addition to the master point carabiners and it is easy to mis-clip the master point. A simpler and more economical way utilizes a single cordelette.

STEP 1 Clip the cordelette into points A, B, and C. (Position the triple fisherman knot between any two points.)

STEP 2 Pull the sections between points A and B, and points B & C down to meet the bottom of the main loop. You will now have three loops.

STEP 3 Overlap the three resulting loops and pre-equalize them in the direction of anticipated force. This forms a triple, common loop. (The one disadvantage to the cordelette is that it is not self-equalizing; it will not adjust as the angle of force changes. It is critical that the common loop is tied so that it is lined up precisely with the anticipated direction of force.)

STEP 4 Tie a figure eight-on-a-bight or an overhand knot in the common loop to form the master point and clip in your carabiners. (Be sure that the triple fisherman knot does not interfere—re-equalize to get it out of the way).

Utilizing a cordelette in this fashion has been the standard anchoring method used by mountain guides for several years and is now catching on with recreational climbers. There are many reasons to recommend it:

• It uses a minimum of equipment.
• It is simple and fast to construct.
• It forms independent, full-strength loops.
• Extension potential is minimized.
• The master point is easily identified (it is too easy to clip into the Magic X incorrectly).
• The cordelette has many other climbing applications and is a vital piece of self-rescue equipment.

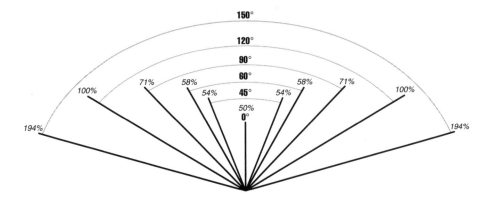

Forces increase as the vector angle increases. Angles greater than 90° should be avoided—lengthen the slings to reduce the angle.

Vectors

A vector is a quantity that has both force and direction. When a climber is hanging on a rope, a vector is created: the weight of the climber is the force and the direction is parallel with the pull of gravity.

Regardless of the method, whenever two anchor points are connected to form a single, equalized unit, an angle is created at the intersection of the two vectors. Because of the possibility of multiplying the forces on the anchor points, climbers should avoid creating vector angles greater than 90°. The following chart shows how the forces are multiplied as the angle between the vectors increases:

Angle of 0°—50% on each anchor
Angle of 45°—54%
Angle of 60°—58%
Angle of 90°—71%
Angle of 120°—100% (with a 150 lb. load, each anchor point holds 150 lbs., for a total weight of 300 lbs.)
Angle of 150°—194% on each anchor point—total weight of 582 lbs.!!!

INTRODUCTION TO THE TOP BELAY

Up to this point we have been using the slingshot system with the rope running up through the top anchor and back to an anchored belayer on the ground. There are times when it is not possible or even ideal to have the belayer on the ground:

- When you want to climb the last pitch of a multi-pitch route. (Imagine trying to rig a slingshot to climb the last pitch of the Salathé Wall!)
- When there is poor or limited access to the bottom of the cliff, like at the sea cliffs of Acadia National Park at high tide.
- When the bottom of the cliff is unsuitable for belaying, nasty talus for instance, or a steep, muddy slope.
- When the route you want to do is longer than half-a-pitch and you only have one rope.

> **Tip #8: You Don't Want Your Belayer On The Ground When...**
>
> - *You want to climb the last pitch of a multi-pitch route*
> - *There is poor or limited access to the bottom of the cliff, like the sea cliffs of Acadia National Park at high tide*
> - *The bottom of the cliff is unsuitable for belaying*
> - *The route you want to do is longer than half-a-pitch and you only have one rope.*

In these cases the belayer will need to be positioned at the top of the cliff. The only basic change in the top belay is in the position of the anchor. In order for the belayer to be oriented correctly between the anchor and the climber (remember your ABCs: Anchor, Belayer, Climber) the master point is not extended over the edge, but built far enough back to leave room for the belayer—typically three-to-eight feet. As always, the belayer should be tied in while building the anchor.

Top belaying involves the following steps:

1. Build an ERNEST anchor positioned for a top belay.
2. The belayer ties into one end of the rope and clips in to the belay anchor using a figure eight loop on the rope. The length of this tether should be adjusted until the desired belayer position is attained.
3. The climber ties in to the other end of the rope.
4. The belayer decides on a belay method (belay device or munter hitch) and the belay position (off the waist, re-directed off the anchor, or off the anchor directly—more on this below) and puts the climber on belay.
5. The belayer then lowers the climber to the base of the climb and belays as the climber ascends back to the anchor. Alternately, if the climber is at the bottom to start, the belayer tosses the rope end down, the climber ties in, is put on belay, and climbs up to the anchor.

The major decision that the climbers need to make is which of three belay options to choose:

1. Belaying directly off the harness.
2. Belaying off the harness and re-directing the rope back through the anchor itself as a directional.
3. Belaying directly off the anchor.

There are four options for belaying from the top belay position:

A. Belaying from the harness with a device.

B. Re-directing the belay through the anchor.

C. Belaying directly off the anchor.

Belaying From The Harness With A Device

This may be the most common, but it is not always the best choice. Its use is appropriate:

- On low-angled slabs.
- When the anchor is in the ideal position for the belayer to catch a fall (behind and slightly above is best, allowing the belayer a natural stance at the edge).
- When the route is within the climber's ability.
- When there is little chance the belayer will have to hold the climber for long periods of time.

Advantages:

- Easy and natural to operate the belay device.
- Affords a very stable position when the belayer is *aligned* and *tight*.
- It is easy to give the climber extra tension (just squat down while taking in the slack, then stand up).

Disadvantages:

- Difficult when repeated falls or long hangs are expected.
- The belayer can lose control of the belay plate if a keeper cord is not used.
- The force on the belay is 2x (x=body weight), the belayer plus the climber.
- Complicates escaping the belay in an emergency.
- Hard to incorporate into a self-rescue system.

Re-directing The Belay Off The Anchor

Appropriate in many circumstances, this is a slingshot belay. Good on most terrain and when the anchor is well-positioned above and behind the belayer.

Advantages:

- Easy and natural to operate the belay device.
- Friction through the master point reduces the load on the belayer's waist.
- The direction of force is certain.
- The anchor does not have to be in the ideal location right behind and above the belayer— the belayer can re-direct off a remote anchor (i.e., from a tree 30 feet back from the edge).
- Easier to escape the belay or incorporate into a self-rescue system.

Disadvantages:

- A hard or unexpected fall could potentially jerk the belayer off balance toward the anchor; the belayer must be braced for a pull toward the anchor, not toward the climber.
- The force on the anchor is 4x.

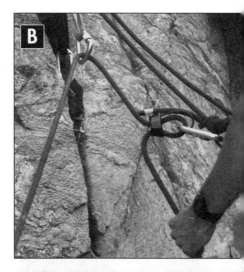

Belaying Directly Off The Anchor

With this method, the belay device is connected directly to the belay anchor and is not attached to the belayer at all. This been standard practice for mountain guides for years. Appropriate on most terrain and when the anchor position allows effective operation.

Advantages:

- The least strenuous: the belayer never holds much of a load, only 0.1 to 0.2 body weight according to the *American Mountain Guides Association Guides Manual.*
- The direction of force is certain.
- Works well with a GriGri or Munter Hitch.
- Can be operated off a remote anchor using the Munter Hitch.
- The force on the anchor is minimal.
- Escaping the belay is simple and quick (the belayer is not connected to the belay system and can block and escape the belay in a matter of seconds).
- Easy to incorporate into a self-rescue system.

Disadvantages:

- Initially, not as natural and takes some getting used to.
- Requires a more sophisticated understanding of the limitations of the various belay devices (belay plates or tubes are usually *not* appropriate).

D. Belaying from an extended master point.

Belaying Directly Off The Anchor Using An Extended Master Point

This method belays directly off the anchor but moves the Master Point down to the just behind the belayer's side. This is accomplished by tying a figure eight on a bight on the live side of the rope just short of the belayer's position. The belay device is then connected to and operated from this loop.

Advantages:

- Any type of belay device may be used (when belaying directly off the anchor when it is out of reach of the belayer, plates and tubes should not be used because they cannot be locked off).
- It is often easier for the belayer to operate the belay device smoothly.
- It offers the same ease and natural operation as belaying directly off the belayers harness yet allows an easy belay escape if necessary.

Disadvantages:

- If the belayer is standing and the climber falls the belay device will be pulled to the ground and control could be lost (clipping the figure eight on a bight loop to the belayer's harness with a short sling will increase security).
- If the new master point is tied too far down the rope, rope stretch may pull the belay device out of reach of the belayer—be sure to tie the figure eight on a bight slightly closer to the main anchor than the belayer's position.

Rappelling

Rappelling is one of the most common climbing activities and, unfortunately, one of the most dangerous. Unlike climbing, where there is a belay backup in case of a fall, rappelling is often carried out without any backup whatsoever. If anything goes wrong and the rappeller loses control, he or she can fall to the ground. Rappelling without a backup is like climbing without a belay—the consequences can be tragic.

"Two climbers, S.H. and W.T. finished climbing the route 'Jolley Rodger' around 14:00 on August 23, and decided to rappel down the route. S.H. would go first, but declined a safety belay which W.T. offered him (emphasis added). A tree was slung with a piece of webbing, the doubled rope was secured to it with two non-locking carabiners, and then S.H. clipped his descender into the rope. But as he leaned back to start the rappel, one side of the rope slid through the anchor carabiners, and S.H. fell some 20 meters to the ground; he had clipped in only one side of the rappel rope. Nearby climbers assisted…and rescue personnel reached the victim within minutes, but S.H. did not survive, and was pronounced dead on arrival at the hospital." (*Accidents in North American Mountaineering,* 1996, page 13.)

Three fundamental rules were broken in this accident: no buddy check of the system, no helmet, and no backup belay. Don't break them yourself.

Though rappelling is sometimes pursued as an activity on its own, most climbers use rappelling as a tool to descend when walking down is impossible or inconvenient. As a tool, rappelling should be used with the utmost care and every precaution should be taken. At toprope areas, rappelling is most often used to:
• Descend to the top of a climb to establish a toprope anchor.
• Descend from a fixed anchor after completing a climb.

Basic Rappel Precautions

The following precautions apply in all rappelling situations, whether a climber is doing one rappel to descend from a route, or a group is rappelling as an activity on its own:
• Be certain there is nothing hanging loose that can become caught in the rappel device: long hair, a helmet chin strap, shirt, slings, skin, etc.
• Establish safety and helmet zones at the top and bottom of the cliff.
• Perform buckle, knot and belay checks.
• Be certain the anchor is *secure*, paying particular attention to padding the edge.
• Have a backup in place, either a separate belay rope or a clamping hitch on the rappeller's harness.
• Consider a chest harness with small children.

The Basic Rappel Setup

The following steps assume an ernest and secure anchor, the use of a figure eight device, plate or tube, and that the climbers are tied in to the anchor while at the edge preparing to rappel.

STEP 1 Double the rope through the master point. Don't always assume that a wrap of tape on the rope has stayed at the midpoint:

"When we examined (his) rope after the accident, we found that the tape originally marking the midpoint was off-center by 25 feet." (*Accidents in North American Mountaineering,* 1995, page 45.)

Doubling the rope only takes a minute or so and should be done even if the rappel is less than half-a-rope-length long. For longer rappels, tie two ropes together and clip the master point at the joining knot. (See the Advanced Knots section for joining knots.)

Tip #9: Basic Rappel Precautions

- Make sure nothing can get caught in the rappel device: long hair, a helmet chin strap, shirt, slings, skin, etc.
- Establish safety zones and helmet zones at both the top and bottom of the cliff.
- Perform buckle & knot checks.
- Be certain the anchor is secure, paying particular attention to padding the edge.
- Have a backup in place, either a separate belay rope or an Autoblock.
- Consider a chest harness with small children.

STEP 2 Tie large knots in the ends of the rope, or ropes, (a figure eight-on-a-bight works well) to eliminate the possibility of rappelling off the end of the rope. This is a good habit to get into even on short rappels onto flat ground. I was guiding one day at a popular toprope crag and watched a party nearby prepare to rappel a 75-foot route. One climber was on the ground and the other was at the top preparing the rappel. I watched as the top climber dropped the rope ends. They became tangled on the ledge and the climber on the ground yelled this fact up to her partner. The top climber could not see the rope. "Tell me when the rope is down," he yelled as he jiggled the rope. The ends popped free and one end piled up on the ground while the other end hung free about 15-feet up. "It's down," the climber on the ground yelled. Obviously this climber did not understand that both ends needed to be on the ground. "On rappel," the upper climber yelled and down he came. As he rappelled the rope stretched so that when he popped off the short end he just dropped a foot or so onto the ground. Neither one of them seemed aware of their close call.

STEP 3 Lap coil the rope and yell, "Rope!" (If other climbers are in the area, wait for "Clear!") Drop the top half of the coil, then the bottom.

STEP 4 Thread the rope through the rappel device and clip to the harness with a locking carabiner or reversed and opposed carabiners. (If the backup will be a clamping hitch off the climber's harness—for maximum effectiveness, extend the device away from the harness with a 24-inch sling girthhitched to the harness.)

STEP 5 Establish a backup with either a separate rope, which can be belayed from the same anchor as the rappel, or a clamping hitch on the rappeller's harness. If there is someone on the ground, that person can give the person rappelling a fireman's belay by holding the rope. It the rappeller loses control, the belayer simply pulls the rope tight, taking the place of the rappeller's brake hand. This is a fast, simple and effective belay. A backup is essential, as the following story will demonstrate:

"Chris went first, and after descending about ten meters, her right foot slipped, sending her swinging against the wall with her right side. Surprised, she made the mistake of releasing the rope with her brake hand in order to steady herself, and she immediately began to fall." (*Accidents in North American Mountaineering*, 1996, page 11.)

She received many scrapes and bruises and third degree rope burns on her hands. This accident could have been avoided with a separate belay or clamping hitch backup.

To set up a clamping hitch backup, use the following steps:
1. As noted in Step 4 above, ideally the rappel device should be extended from the harness by girth hitching a standard 24-inch sling through the climber's harness.
2. Attach a locking carabiner to the harness on the same side that the breaking hand will be on and clip a short prussik loop to it (either a cord or a standard 24-inch sling will work well).
3. Wrap the sling around the rappel rope toward the belay device—typically three-to-five wraps depending on the amount of braking power desired—then clip it back to the carabiner and lock it. As the climber rappels he or she should hold the clamping hitch loosely in the brake hand. If he or she lets go of the brake hand, the clamping hitch will grab the rope and stop the rappel. The clamping hitch works by taking the place of the brake hand. Because this requires little holding power, the clamping hitch will still be easy to loosen after being weighted: simply grab the knot and give a sharp downward tug. This works great when you wish to stop frequently while on rappel to do something that requires two hands, like cleaning quickdraws off protection bolts. A Prussik, Klemheist or Autoblock can be used in this application. (See page 52.)

Basic Rappelling

The key to safe rappelling is maintaining control throughout the process. Building an *ernest* and *secure* anchor, establishing a backup system, and taking basic precautions like tying knots in the end of the rope provide a solid foundation and go a long way in avoiding accidents. Once the climber starts over the edge, other precautions need to be taken to ensure that control is maintained until the climber reaches the ground:
• Correct body position is critical throughout the rappel. The ideal position is with the legs perpendicular to the rock, feet shoulder-width apart, the torso vertical, the brake hand on

the hip, and the guide hand loosely on the rope above the rappel device. The transition over the edge is the hardest part: try to use footholds and keep any backup belay ropes tight.

- While rappelling, keep the feet shoulder-width apart with heels on the cliff, and stay directly below the anchor to reduce potential swing.
- Keep the brake hand on the hip. If you let your hand creep up to the belay device the rope can suck skin and fingers into the device, making for a nasty and potentially dangerous pinch.
- If additional friction is desired the rope can be passed behind the rappeller's waist and the brake applied with the other hand.
- Step carefully over overhangs.
- When the ground is reached, immediately remove the belay device from the rope and shout, "Off rappel!"

TOPROPING ROUTES LONGER THAN HALF-A-ROPE LENGTH USING THE SLINGSHOT BELAY

Sometimes it is advantageous to use the slingshot on longer routes. This can be accomplished by tying two ropes together. Unfortunately, this can mean passing the joining knot while the climber is still climbing—a potentially dangerous procedure. The following method will allow any route up to a full pitch in length to be toproped using the slingshot belay and without passing the knot. This brilliant method was first described to me by Alain Comeau:

- Tie two ropes together.
- Position the knot joining the two ropes on the belayer's side of the master point.
- The belayer closes the system by tying in to the end of the belay rope.
- The climber ties in to the rope at the point where it reaches the ground, not at the end. The easiest tie-in method is to run a loop through the climber's harness, tie a double fisherman around the live strand and clip the loop formed back into the climber's harness with a locking carabiner. Other appropriate methods include using a double figure eight-on-a-bight, a bowline-on-a-bight (both backed up with half-a-double fisherman). Any leftover slack will be trailed behind the climber.
- The belayer attaches the belay device to the rope at the point where it reaches the ground.
- When properly set up, the knot joining the two ropes will be at the anchor and exactly halfway between the climber and the belayer. The climber will reach the anchor at the same time that the joining knot reaches the belayer—no knot pass will be needed and the belayer can lower the climber as usual.

TOPROPING OVERHANGING OR TRAVERSING ROUTES

It is often possible to set up effective topropes on gently over-hanging or traversing routes. The following method will max-imize safety. Because overhanging or traversing routes add a swinging element to the picture, each route should be care-fully analyzed to make certain that it can be climbed with a reasonable margin of safety. Regarding traversing routes in particular, the following method is only for those routes requiring a minimum number of directional anchors.

Equipping The Route

Check the swing for potential dangers to a falling climber (for example, a tree out from the base that might be hit, or a ledge that a swinging climber could fall onto). I once ignored this important step while climbing in a gym in Reno, Nevada. I was the third to lead a severely overhanging 5.10c route and the only one to climb it without falling. After clipping the anchor my partners taunted me with, "Bet you can't down-climb it." With my honor at stake I shut off my normally cau-tious brain and accepted the challenge. I began downclimbing with an overhead toprope but did not bother to re-clip any of the bolts. I huffed and puffed my way down, oblivious to the tremendous swing potential that was developing. Near the bottom I heard the belayer, John, say something like, "Whoa, I'm taking him off belay, that way he won't swing, let's give him a spot." I made it down safely, and when I turned around I saw what was making them all nervous—thirty feet behind the climb was a vertical steel girder that held up the roof. We figured it out, and yes, I would have hit it.

After the anchor is established, to equip the route, either rappel or lower down the route, clipping bolts or placing gear every few feet. If placing gear, be certain that its strongest ori-entation is in line with the anticipated direction of force. If the route is quite steep, it may not be easy to swing in to clip each piece. By using an anchor at the base of the route the belayer can help the climber equip the route as follows:

STEP 1 Establish a directional anchor as near to the base of the route as possible and clip the belay rope to it. If the route is bolted, the first bolt may be used if it can be reached easi-ly and safely.

STEP 2 The climber equipping the route clips a quickdraw into the harness and then into the rope between the anchor and the belayer. As the climber is lowered, he or she will be kept in close to the route by the taught rope.

STEP 3 The belayer stops the climber each time a protection point is reached. The climber clips a quickdraw into the protection and then into the rope above the tie-in knot.

STEP 4 When the climber reaches the ground, the belay rope should now run from the belayer, through the direction-al anchor at the base of the route, up to the main anchor, and then back down the route through all the quickdraws to the climber. The next climber will climb on the side running through the quickdraws.

As each climber ascends the route, he or she unclips the protection as it is reached. (Do not climb past the protection or you will be leading and risking a dangerous fall.) After reaching the top, the climber is lowered back down the route and repeats Steps 2 and 3. The last climber cleans the protection.

LOWERING FROM A FIXED ANCHOR

Double-bolt anchors with chains and lowering links are very common. When using a slingshot belay off these anchors the last person must clean the slings and lower or rappel. This transition is potentially dangerous. The following will help minimize the risk:

1. If the anchor is easily accessible from above, the best method is to have the last person simply lower off. Someone can go back up to dismantle the anchor. It may be appropriate for the last climber to climb over the top and then dismantle the anchor. Tying in while working at the edge is highly recommended.

2. If the last climber is going to lower off the anchor, it should be pre-rigged with either a Magic X or quickdraws. This master point should be above the fixed lowering ring. When the rope is threaded through the master point, pass it through the lowering ring as well. (The lowering ring acts as a backup.) As climbers ascend, each will be belayed and lowered off the master point. Be sure the rope runs freely.

3. When the last climber reaches the top, he or she unclips the slings and lowers off the fixed link. At no time will the climber be off belay.

Lowering From A Fixed Anchor

A. The climber has reached the anchor.

B. The climber has girth hitched two slings to his harness and clipped one to each bolt (do not clip into only one bolt).

If the anchor does not allow for pre-rigging—it may be two bolts that can be lowered off directly—do the following:

1. Rig as usual with a Magic X or quick draws.
2. The last climber should clip into the anchor with a sling that is girth hitched to the harness. The climber can either clip directly into the master point or clip into the bolts themselves. Do not clip into just one bolt or coldshut.
3. While still on belay, pull up five feet of slack, tie a backup figure eight-on-a-bight, and clip it to the harness with a carabiner. This prevents accidentally dropping the rope.
4. Double-check your anchors and then untie the figure eight on the harness completely.
5. Pass the rope through the bolts (the hangers must be the kind that can be lowered off directly) and tie back into the harness.
6. Unclip and untie the backup figure eight, pull up to the anchor, and have the belayer take in all the slack and lock you off.
7. Remove the Magic X or quickdraws and lower off.

C: The climber has tied a figure eight tie-in knot, passed it through the bolts and tied back into his harness.(Only bolt hangers designed for lowering, like these Metolius bolts, should be used in this fashion.)

D: The climber has unclipped the figure eight backup, removed the girth-hitched slings and is ready to be lowered.

A. The climber has arrived at the anchor, clipped into the bolts with slings and is ready to be lowered.

B. The climber has untied his figure eight tie-in knot, passed the rope through the anchor, and tied the second figure eight backup on the short end of the rope.

RAPPELLING FROM A FIXED ANCHOR

If you decide to rappel the route when done climbing, use the following procedure:

1. When the last climber arrives at the anchor, clip in to either the master point or the anchor bolts with a sling(s) and locking carabiner(s). Call "Off belay!"
2. Pull up ten feet of slack, tie a figure eight knot and clip it into the anchor or harness to prevent accidentally dropping it while rigging the rappel.
3. Untie the figure eight tie-in knot on the harness, pass the rope through the lowering ring, lap link, or appropriate bolt hangers, and pull all the slack through until the backup figure eight is reached.
4. Tie a new backup knot in the tail end of the rope, clip it in.
5. Untie the first backup knot and pull the rope through the anchor until the middle of the rope is reached.
6. Untie the second backup knot and drop the rope.
7. Have the climber on the ground test-pull the rope, and modify the rope's position as necessary.
8. Attach the rappel device to the rope and clamping hitch backup (if a fireman's belay is used you can dispense with the clamping hitch).
9. Pull up to the anchor, remove slack from between the anchor and the rappel device, and either lock off the clamping hitch or have the belayer activate the fireman's belay.
10. Remove the anchor slings, store them properly so they can't get caught in the rappel device, and rappel.

ADVANCED CLIMBING OPTIONS

With sufficient expertise, toproping can be an excellent tool to practice more advanced techniques with minimal risk. Feel free to use your imagination as long as you follow the basic *ernest*, *secure*, and *catch* principles.

Lead Practice

Leading can be easily simulated on toprope. A slingshot system is built and the climber ascends with the standard overhead belay, trailing a second rope, placing protection and clipping in as progress is made. The toprope can be kept a little loose as long as safety is not compromised. The second climber can follow the pitch, also on a toprope, and critique each placement before it is removed. This can make a fun and educational game, with each climber taking a turn at simulated "leading," placing both good and bad pieces for the "second" to critique. Another option is for the climber to stop somewhere on the pitch, build an anchor, and rappel using the second rope. For more on leading, consult *How to Rock Climb, 3rd Edition* (Falcon Press: Helena, MT, 1998), *Advanced Rock Climbing* (Chockstone: Evergreen, CO, 1997) and *Mountaineering: Freedom of the Hills, 6th edition* (The Mountaineers, 1997).

Aid Climbing Practice

Using the same set-up as for lead practice, you can practice aid climbing. No other method is as good for teaching the nuances of placing protection. Anchoring, ascending fixed ropes and hauling systems can also be practiced. *Big Walls!* (Chockstone: Evergreen, CO, 1994) will give you the techniques needed for climbing the big aid routes of the world.

C. The climber has untied the first figure eight backup, pulled the rope through to the middle, untied the second figure eight backup and dropped the end. The belayer has determined that the rope will pull through the anchor.

D. The climber has attached the rappel device, established a backup (fireman's belay in this case), removed the girth hitched slings and is beginning the rappel.

Self-Rescue Practice

Some self-rescue techniques can be practiced on a toprope, but extra caution should be taken. When practicing belay escapes or raising systems, consider using a heavy pack as the load to minimize the risk. If a climber is to be the load, practice as close to the ground as possible. Just a foot or two up is often all that is needed to get the hang of the system. Check out David Fasulo's classic, *Self-Rescue* (Falcon Press: Helena, MT, 1998).

Woman's Rock Day in North Conway, NH. In any group there will be those who are naturally good climbers and those who are not. Be sure there's a route everyone can do.   S. Peter Lewis

Group
Management

Supervising a toprope site is a challenging job. Whether you are volunteering at a summer camp, working as a professional mountain guide, or just introducing a group of your friends to climbing for the first time, the responsibility can weigh heavily. Basic group management techniques will help maintain control and reduce the risks as well as your anxiety level.

When approaching the subject of group management it is important to remember that most people who you take out to the crag will be unfamiliar with mountain terrain, and thus often unaware of even the most fundamental hazards.

The keys to group management are:
1. Prepare and organize.
2. Keep the group together.
3. Minimize hazards.
4. Keep participants occupied.

PREPARE AND ORGANIZE

1. Have a detailed plan and schedule for the day's activities. Have enough planned to prevent boredom (which leads to trouble) but also plan on some "down time" to re-charge.
2. Have a group equipment checklist and take inventory at both the beginning and the end of the day: "Ropes, we don't have ropes?"
3. Provide participants with a personal equipment list and be sure they have everything before starting out.
4. Consider bringing a larger "group" first aid kit instead of just your personal kit.
5. Be certain that you are not the only one who knows where the keys to the van and the emergency contact telephone numbers are located.

KEEP THE GROUP TOGETHER

1. On approaches and descents use a leader in front and a sweeper in the rear to keep the group together.
2. Re-group at all trail junctions.
3. Even if the destination is known, no one should travel alone.
4. Pace the group based on the comfort level of the slowest member—rushing is fatiguing and can dampen enthusiasm. A large group can be split into fast and slow subgroups if there are enough leaders.

MINIMIZE HAZARDS—AT THE MACRO AND MICRO LEVEL

1. On approaches and descents, alert the group to every possible hazard. Remember, novices may not even be aware that wet leaves are slippery.
2. At the site, designate safety zones that the group must stay within. Use visual boundaries such as trees, boulders, etc., or consider using a spare rope to cordon off danger areas—cliff edges for instance.
3. Set a bouldering height limit and don't let people boulder where others are climbing.
4. Designate a helmet zone. It should extend out from the base at least as far as the cliff is high. Consider requiring helmets to be worn on the approach, especially if it involves talus. I was observing a toprope class one day in Arizona; we were on a second class approach that wound through big talus blocks below the crag. It was easy going but you had to do some rock-hopping and keep your balance. At one point everyone had to take a long step over a big hole and onto a canted boulder and then make a couple of scramble moves to get back on easy ground. Though the participants all had helmets, most of them were just carrying them in their hands. Two girls approached the step-across move and stopped. They looked into the hole. One of them turned to the other and said a little anxiously, "I'm putting on my helmet." "Me too," the other said. The group leaders were nowhere to be seen. Both girls made the move easily. But what if they hadn't?
5. If people will be moving between the base and the top and there is any possibility that they could stray into dangerous terrain, flag the path. (Remove the flags at the end of the day).
6. If rappelling is to be the main activity, keep a monitor at the bottom as well as the top.
7. If competent adults are part of the group, especially those who you can trust to belay, put them to work.

KEEP PARTICIPANTS OCCUPIED

1. Keep instructor-to-participant ratios within manageable limits, depending on the age and experience of the participants: 1:4 is a suggested maximum if no counselors are available. Lower ratios keep more people busy at any one time.
2. Use backup belayers whenever possible. This is especially important with youth.
3. Provide alternative activities such as bouldering, which requires at least of two spotters (teach them how to spot, and set a height limit); or anchor-building. Other activities may also be chosen, depending on the interest and responsibility levels of the participants. Keep track of your gear!

A SPECIAL MESSAGE ABOUT YOUTH

Young people may be the most challenging group to manage—they seem bent on endangering themselves. Here are some pointers on keeping a group of them safely active:

- Young people have amazingly short attention spans. Plan activities with short bursts of intense action and as much "hands on" stuff as possible—long lectures are out.
- Be as concise and clear as possible with directions and warnings: repeat them frequently and give them information only on a "need-to-know" basis.
- Be demonstrative with hazard warnings. Instead of telling someone his or her feet may slip if they're too low on a rappel, show them. A demonstration I always liked was to take a dry stick, balance it between a couple of rocks, and say, "This is your femur." Then drop another rock on it and say, "This is your femur if your belayer lets go of his brake hand." It's very effective.
- Give everyone a job to do, such as backing up a belay.
- If possible, keep yourself free to float and keep track of the big picture.
- Require knot, buckle, and belay checks before leaving the ground.
- Keep the humor and laughter levels high—it's impossible to be bored when you're laughing.
- Use cheerleaders. Young people are easily discouraged by struggle, and easily encouraged by praise from their peers. Instill a desire among the whole group to see that everyone succeeds.
- In any group there will be those who are naturally good climbers and those who are not. You will not be the only one to notice this—the weaker climbers will notice too. Be sure that there is a route that everyone can do and cheer loudest when the fat kid gets up the 5.1.
- Take periodic head counts.
- Require that they ask permission to leave the group (for example, to go to the bathroom) and check back in when they return.
- Make sure everyone has enough to eat and drink—bring extra.

Tip #10: Keys To Managing Groups

- *Prepare and organize.*
- *Keep the group together.*
- *Minimize hazards.*
- *Keep participants occupied.*

Glossary

Active Protection	A protection device with moving parts; also known as an SLCD.
American Triangle	A dangerous webbing anchor formed by threading a single piece of webbing through two anchors and tying the ends together. This forms a triangle whose vectors multiply the force on the anchors. Commonly found on fixed anchors.
AMGA	<u>A</u>merican <u>M</u>ountain <u>G</u>uides <u>A</u>ssociation is a national nonprofit organization that trains and certifies professional mountain guides and accredits guiding companies.
Anchor	A temporary, secure point that a climber uses for protection from injury during a fall. Usually capable of holding several thousand pounds and can come in many forms including: trees, boulders, pitons, bolts, chocks, camming devices, etc.
Belay	"To hold." This refers to a system of devices and techniques that combine to protect a climber from being injured in a fall by locking the rope.
Belay Anchor	Any single-point or multipoint anchor that is used to belay from.
Belay Escape	Any of several methods that allow the belayer to tie off a fallen climber and physically leave the climbing system.
Belay/Rappel Device	Any of several types of metal devices that are used to create manageable friction on a rope for belaying or rappelling.
Bight	A bend in the rope used in many knots and to thread belay/rappel devices.
Body Harness	Any combination of a waist harness and a chest harness—can be purchased complete or improvised.
Bolt	A metal shaft that is placed in a drilled hole and is held there either by friction or epoxy. An accompanying hanger provides an attachment point—designed to be loaded perpendicular to the shaft.
Bombproof	An anchor judged by a climber to be very secure.
Brake Hand	The hand that holds the rope on the side of the belay device opposite the climber and that will activate the locking mechanism. The brake hand never leaves the rope.
Cairn	A pile of stones used to mark a trail.
Carabiner	An aluminum snap-link used to connect parts of a climbing system.
Chock	Generic for "artificial chockstone." Any of many designs of passive protection that rely on wedging in a constriction for security: Hexes, Stoppers, Lowe Tricams, etc.
Chockstone	A stone wedged in a crack.
Clamping Hitch	Any of several hitches that will tighten and lock when loaded—most often used on a rope to temporarily hold a load.

Closed System	A contained system. The belayer tying into the end of the rope forms a "closed system" that will keep the climber from being dropped. The Magic X forms a "closed system" wherein the master point is attached to the sling and not merely looped over it.
Cord	Nylon fibers woven like a rope with kernmantle construction. Typically 5.5 to 8mm in diameter. Tied in short loops as clamping hitches.
Cordelette	A six- to nine-foot loop of cord tied with a double or triple fisherman's knot and usually between 5.5 and 8 mm in diameter. Has many uses including building belay anchors and as a component of self-rescue systems.
Core	The rope's central core of woven nylon fibers. It accounts for about 85 per cent of the rope's strength.
Directional	Any auxiliary anchor point used to position the rope in the strongest possible location.
Downclimbing	Climbing a route from the top down.
Double-pass Buckle	The standard harness buckle that requires the waistbelt webbing to be threaded through twice, crossing over itself and locking on the second pass.
Dynamic	In the context of climbing it means any part of a system that will yield or move when activated, typically reducing forces. During a fall, knots tighten and the belayer moves, making the belay "dynamic."
Dynamic Rope	A climbing rope that is designed to stretch considerably and absorb the force of a falling climber. The only kind of rope suitable for leading.
Equalization	Any of several methods that tie anchors together in such a way that they share a load equally.
Extension	A potential slipping of components in an anchor system to adjust for the failure of any point. This causes an undesirable shock load.
Fall Factor	A measure of the severity of a fall derived by dividing the length of the fall into the length of rope in the system: the maximum fall factor is two.
Figure 8 Device	An aluminum rappel and belay device in the shape of an "8."
Figure 8 Knot	A knot shaped like an "8" that has many uses including: connecting the rope to the harness, tying in to an anchor, tying two ropes together, etc.
Fireman's Belay	A rappel belay created by having a person at the bottom of a pitch hold the rappel rope. Keeping the rope slack allows the rappeller to descend; pulling down on the rope locks off the rappel.
Fixed Anchor	Any permanent anchor point. Can be natural, like a tree, or man-made, like a bolt or piton.
Free Climbing	Climbing where the hands and feet are used to make progress and climbing equipment is used only to provide protection in the case of a fall. See also "Soloing."
GriGri	A mechanical belay device with a cam that rotates and grabs the rope when loaded and aids the belayer in catching a fall.

Guide Hand	The hand opposite the brake hand. It helps position and manage the rope.
Helmet Zone	An area whose boundaries are determined by the group leader, where helmets are required to be worn.
Hex	A non-symmetrical, five-sided chock with varying degrees of camming action.
HMS Carabiner	Any large, pear-shaped carabiner with a large, round curve on the end opposite the gate hinge. This is the only type of carabiner that should be used with the Munter Hitch.
Horn	A spike of rock.
IFMGA	The International Federation of Mountain Guide Associations is a nonprofit organization that sets standards and certifies mountain guides worldwide. Membership is made up of countries and their representative mountain guiding associations.
Impact Force	The force still remaining when a falling climber comes to a stop. In a severe fall it can be a maximum of 2,680 lbs.
Improvised Ascending	Any one of various methods for ascending a fixed rope without the use of mechanical rope clamps.
Keeper Cord	A short cord attached to a belay/rappel device. It keeps the device within reach when in use, and clips the device to a carabiner when not in use.
Keeper Knot	Any auxiliary knot used to ensure the security of another knot, (e.g., half-a-double fisherman's knot tied after the figure eight tie-in as a keeper knot).
Lap Coil	A coil that consists of overlapping loops, typically tied off so it can be carried like a backpack. It is less likely to tangle when being uncoiled for use.
Lead Climbing	A system of climbing from the ground up wherein a climber ascends belayed from below by a partner, trailing a rope and clipping it through intermediate protection points. In the case of a fall, the belayer will hold the fall, which will be caught by the last piece of protection. The leader will anchor the rope at the end of the pitch and belay up the second climber on a toprope. The process is then repeated until the top of a climb is reached.
Live End	The end of the rope tied to the climber.
Locking Carabiner	A carabiner with any of various locking mechanisms that keep the gate from opening unexpectedly.
Lowe Tricam	A single cam with a pivot point, opposing rails, and a fixed sling that follows the curve of the cam between the rails. It works by camming or wedging in a crack or pocket.
Lowering	A method of descent wherein the climber weights the rope and is let down by the belayer. The most common method of descent from a slingshot belay.
Magic X	A method for creating a self-equalizing master point by tying two anchor points together with a sling loop. A half-twist in one strand of the sling creates a closed system ensuring that the master point cannot come off the rope if either anchor point fails.

Multidirectional	An anchor that is secure in any direction.
Multipitch	A climb that is longer than the length of a climbing rope and must be climbed in stages.
Munter Hitch	A hitch that binds on itself creating manageable friction. Used for belaying and rappelling.
Master Point	The central attachment point in a belay anchor.
Quickdraw	A short sling with a carabiner clipped to each end.
Passive Protection	A protection device without moving parts—a chock.
Pitch	A section of a climb whose maximum length is dictated by the length of the rope, usually 50 meters. All toprope climbs are one pitch.
Piton	Any one of several designs of steel spikes from the size of a postage-stamp to 6 inches that are hammered in to cracks to create an anchor. The eye provides an attachment point, usually loaded perpendicular to its long axis.
Protection	A single anchor that the rope runs freely through to protect a climber during a lead.
Rappel	Any of various methods of descending a rope using controlled friction.
Rappel Ring/Link	A permanent ring or lap-link found at the master point of a fixed anchor that the rope is threaded through for rappelling or lowering.
Re-direct	Changing the direction of a vector by re-routing it. This can increase control (e.g., running the rope from the belayer's device through an anchor before going to the climber).
Reversed & Opposed	Two carabiners that are used together are oriented with their gates opening in opposite directions and on opposite sides. Used any time maximum security is required.
Rope Drag	Friction caused by the rope running through parts of the climbing system.
Round Coil	Traditional circular coil, carried over one's head and a shoulder.
Safety Zone	An area whose boundaries are determined by the group leader, that participants are required to stay within to maintain control and maximize the safety of the group.
Sandbag	To mislead someone regarding the difficulty or danger of a route. Potentially dangerous.
Self-equalizing	An anchor that maintains equalization automatically when its master point is re-positioned: the Magic X is a self-equalizing anchor.
Self-rescue	Any rescue system utilizing only the climbing equipment that the climbers on the scene possess.
Sharp End	A climber leading a route and taking the associated risks is said to be on the "sharp end."
Sheath	The woven, nylon outer layer of a rope that protects the core from damage. It accounts for about 15 per cent of the strength of the rope.

SLCD	Spring Loaded Camming Device describes the design of several brands of active protection that use spring-loaded cams to create an anchor in a crack.
Sling	Webbing tied or sewn into a loop. Typically 4 inches to 72 inches long.
Slingshot Belay	The standard system for toproping where the rope is doubled through an anchor at the top of the route and the climber is belayed from on the ground.
Soloing	Climbing without a belay. A fall can be—and often is—fatal.
Stacking The Rope	Uncoiling the rope into a loose pile with the top and bottom exposed: the climber ties into the top end. Propoer stacking minimizes tangles.
Standing End	The opposite end of the rope from the one the climber is tied to. See Live End.
Static Rope	A climbing rope that is designed to stretch very little and is used in situations where only body-weight loads are expected: rappelling and ascending fixed ropes.
Stopper	Any of several wedge-shaped chocks designed to fit constrictions in cracks.
Talus	Large rocks (6 inches or bigger) that are often present on the slopes underneath cliffs. Caution is required while moving over talus because the stability varies.
Thread	Any naturally occurring tunnel in the rock that a sling may be passed through and used as an anchor (if strong enough).
Toproping	Any of several systems wherein the climber is protected from falling by an overhead belay.
Tri-axial Loading	A dangerous situation that arises when a carabiner is stressed by three vectors, one of which is not aligned with the carabiner's long axis. This weakens the carabiner and can cause failure if shock-loaded.
UIAA	The Union Internationale Des Associations Alpines is the international agency that sets standards and tests climbing safety equipment.
Uni-directional	An anchor that is secure only in one direction.
Vector	Any quantity with both force and direction (e.g., a climber hanging on a rope forms a vector between himself and the anchor).
Waist Belay	A belay method that uses the belayer's body to create the friction necessary to hold the climber. Its use is limited to low-load situations.
Walking	The tendency for SLCDs to creep, cams first, into a crack when lateral force is applied to their stem. This can compromise the security of the placement and can be minimized by using a sling extension.
Webbing	Nylon fibers woven flat like a strap. Used for making slings.

Index

T

U, V, W, X, Y and Z